OF DIVINE WARNING

◆

THE RADICAL IMAGINATION SERIES
Edited by Henry A. Giroux and Stanley Aronowitz

Beyond the Spectacle of Terrorism: Global Uncertainty and the Challenge of the New Media, by Henry A. Giroux (2006)

Global Modernity, by Arif Dirlik (2006)

Left Turn: Forging a New Political Future, by Stanley Aronowitz (2006)

Stormy Weather: Katrina and the Politics of Disposability, by Henry A. Giroux (2006)

The Politics of Possibility: Encountering the Radical Imagination, edited by Gary A. Olson and Lynn Worsham (2007)

The University in Chains: Confronting the Military-Industrial-Academic Complex, by Henry A. Giroux (2007)

Guys and Guns Amok: Domestic Terrorism and School Shootings from the Oklahoma City Bombing to the Virginia Tech Massacre, by Douglas Kellner (2008)

Against Schooling: Toward an Education That Matters, by Stanley Aronowitz (2008)

Of Divine Warning: Reading Disaster in the Modern Age, by Jane Anna Gordon and Lewis R. Gordon (2009)

Forthcoming

Theory from the South: Or, How Euro-America Is Evolving Toward Africa, by Jean Comaroff and John L. Comaroff

OF DIVINE WARNING

READING DISASTER IN THE MODERN AGE

JANE ANNA GORDON AND LEWIS R. GORDON

Routledge
Taylor & Francis Group

LONDON AND NEW YORK

First published 2009 by Paradigm Publishers

Published 2016 by Routledge
2 Park Square, Milton Park, Abingdon, Oxon OX14 4RN
711 Third Avenue, New York, NY 10017, USA

*Routledge is an imprint of the Taylor & Francis Group,
an informa business*

Library of Congress Cataloging-in-Publication Data

Gordon, Jane Anna ,1976–
   Of divine warning : reading disaster in the modern age / Jane Anna
Gordon and Lewis R. Gordon.
     p. cm. — (The radical imagination series)
   Includes bibliographical references (p. 145) and index.
   ISBN 978-1-59451-538-5 (hardcover : alk. paper)
   1. Disasters. 2. Disasters in literature. I. Gordon, Lewis R. (Lewis
Ricardo), 1962– II. Title.
   D24.G754 2009
   303.48'5—dc22

                                                              2009014136

Designed and Typeset by Straight Creek Bookmakers.

ISBN 13: 978-1-59451-538-5 (hbk)
ISBN 13: 978-1-59451-539-2 (pbk)

To Jean and John Comaroff and to their grandchildren,
Mathieu, Jennifer, Sula, and Elijah Gordon
and Mila Bea Comaroff Wang Mi

◇

Contents

◇

Acknowledgments

We dedicate this book to Jean Comaroff and John Comaroff, who have devoted their lives to the study of culture and history, because we here offer teleological suspensions of philosophy and political science through drawing considerably upon resources from anthropology, history, and sociology in addition to other disciplines across the social sciences and humanities. By "teleological suspensions," we mean going beyond the presumption of the completeness of the methods in our own disciplines, with the expectation that they must adjust and develop to illuminate reality rather than expecting reality to conform to them. This does not mean that we reject philosophy and political science but instead that we appreciate the resources offered by many disciplines, including anthropology, history, and sociology, in the study of the human world. One of us has been having conversations on these matters with the Comaroffs since she was able to speak, and the other joined in more than a decade ago. This book is, in a way, a testament to what our unique training in classics, educational theory, history, philosophy, political science, and religious studies brings to that ongoing, lively discussion.

We would like to thank Kenneth Saltman, who initiated our joint reflection on these themes in his anthology *Schooling and the Politics of Disaster.* Although our concerns with education have occupied us for most of our adult lives, we benefited greatly from the experience of working with him on that project. We are grateful for the opportunity to have presented some of what is included in this book in a variety of colloquia and conferences at such institutions as the Center for Afro-Oriental Studies at the Federal University of Bahia in Brazil, Columbia University, Lehman College, Marquette University, La Maison des Sciences de l'Homme in Paris, Lewis University, Northern Illinois University, the Ohio Valley Philosophy of Education Society, Oxford University, Tel-Aviv University, the University of California at Berkeley, the

University of California at Irvine, the University of Cape Town, the University of Natal at Durban-Westville, the University of Maine, the University of Paris VII, the University of the West Indies at Cave Hill in Barbados and at Mona in Jamaica, York University and MacMaster University in Canada, and Temple University where we had co-organized a set of Halloween Lectures and the annual meetings of the Caribbean Philosophical Association.

We also want to thank Henry Giroux and Susan Searls Giroux for the wonderful dialogue over the past ten years and projects that led to our working with Dean Birkenkamp. We have found Birkenkamp's dedication to the publication of work of high intellectual quality and integrity inspiring. Thank you, Dean, also for your appreciation of the continued importance of and genuine love for books. We also want to thank Paget Henry, with whom we have had many Sunday night conversations on social thought, philosophy, political economy, and world events after meals he generously bought from Kabob & Curry; Jean-Paul Rocchi, for the many hours under the cherry tree in Corsica; Drucilla Cornell, Marilyn Nissim-Sabat, and Charles Nissim-Sabat, for the spirited discussions on philosophy, existential psychology, culture, and politics; Gary Schwartz and Heinrich von Staaden, for their wisdom as classicists and educators; Myron Beasley and Stephen Haymes, for conversations on culture, education, food, and performance; and our graduate students, with whom teaching is always an experience of learning.

As always, we thank Mathieu, Jennifer, Sula, and Elijah for their patience as we continue to negotiate the life of the mind and the supervening love we have for them as their parents.

—Jane and Lewis Gordon,
Providence, Rhode Island

◇

Beginning

Looming and unfolding disasters seem these days to be all around. Their frequency, scope, and ultimate meaning are the cause and subject of global anxiety. One need not actively expect an impending apocalypse to consider the future with a sense of foreboding.

There has been much public discussion about the spate of disasters that ushered in the twenty-first century: earthquakes on the seafloor that triggered the 2004 Indian Ocean tsunami abruptly ended, injured, or displaced the lives of almost 230,000 people in thirteen countries;[1] Hurricane Katrina struck the southeastern coast of the United States in 2005; and the Nargis Cyclone, considered the second deadliest named cyclone of all time, touched down in Myanmar in 2008 only ten days before the 7.9 magnitude earthquake on land that killed more than 69,000 people and left millions more injured or homeless in the Sichuan Province of China. More mundanely, in richer countries that once invested in their public infrastructure, bridges are collapsing and steam pipes exploding. In addition, armed violence conducted both by the private and official armies of nations and on behalf of subnational groups multiply. Some of these groups deliberately aim to discredit, others simply to test, the ongoing feasibility of more familiar approaches to solving conflicts politically. The superpowers suffered blows to their sense of security through disastrous consequences of failed or ill-equipped reconnaissance agencies, as the attacks on the Twin Towers in the United States in 2001, subsequent attacks in Spain and England, and the catastrophic military efforts in the Middle East and East Africa attest. As we are told ad infinitum that a triumphalist market fundamentalism, the supposed basis of military defense of that way of life, is the economic end of history, its regular failures and crises near the end of the first decade of the new millennium have left many

1

people in North America and Europe unable to keep their homes and jobs, with a ripple effect from north to south, east to west.

The world of scholarship has not ignored these developments. Many studies, good and bad, explored the causes, effects, meaning, and understanding of disaster from a variety of disciplinary perspectives, and in the past decade many creative courses were introduced and expanded in the academic world, including more professionally enticing ones in disaster management, disaster recovery, and the economic study of disaster.

Our aim is neither to criticize this growing area of research nor cover well-trod terrain. What we offer here is an interpretation of the meaning and significance of disaster that we hope will accentuate the insights in some of the best work in the field, illuminate the broader significance of disaster in recent times, and offer some orientation toward a better understanding of its dynamics for the future. To that end we pose a series of questions across the six chapters below:

What is the significance of disaster?

What is signified by disastrous beings?

Is it possible to decolonize the creatures affected by such significations?

What happens when such creatures no longer speak or are able to speak only under very limited conditions?

What is to be learned from the ruins left by disaster?

And in what sense is it possible to move forward in an age of ruin?

We begin with the ancient understanding of disaster as exemplified by "ill-fated stars" or bodies fallen from the heavens. These movements downward, we contend, although experienced as events in themselves, are also and more importantly signs, symptoms of other phenomena that we would do well to ponder, after a moment's pause, with humility. More frequently the appearance of the signs occasion dread as they collapse into horrible events in themselves, as causes rather than symptoms. The frightened often do not respond to such signs as posing questions that must be answered or as dilemmas demanding a response. This failure to heed warning signs is catastrophic; it is to turn, as did the ill-fated stars, downward. Such a path swallows up what could curb or contain the wave of disaster and destruction. This failure to read and, in so doing, to develop a viable response turns signs into what we call *sign continua* of the disaster of which they warned. They become part of the destructive tide, allowing initial events to cast larger shadows and to create disastrous people and projects. The latter, we argue, includes attacks on any efforts to solve problems politically rather than through the assertion of economically profitable order and rule or simply the metaphysical appeals of hope and luck.

One response to survivors of disaster, we observe, is to treat them as monsters, creatures of admonition, that present us with choices that we must make in spite of the anxiety and uncertainty they provoke. Monsters, those creatures that have plagued human communities since primordial times, are so enduring that they call for the mythopoetic understanding of no less than the underlying source of dread—namely, the disclosure of the self or community to itself. They prod all of us to confront what we would rather not confront. Such creatures are, thus, symptomatic. They are signs that *something* has gone wrong. Among the ancients, monsters were understood to be products of conflicts among the gods and often functioned either as or instruments of sacrifices. Their slaying or incineration would restore the community, setting things right, or they would root out the culprit who was the additional source of pollution. This role for the monster was displaced in the modern age of naturalistic rationalization. Monsters became beings with an inner nature that was against nature: They became natural deviants, and without a telos or purpose of directed goodness in the world, their presence occasioned crises of values and the threat of nihilism. Our first two chapters address the movements from disaster to disastrous beings, to monstrosities.

The succeeding two chapters further explore the generation of modern disastrous people, first in Mary Shelley's *Frankenstein* and then through more systematic and widespread processes of colonization and enslavement. Shelley's creature, like many other far older ones, was eloquent, offering reflections upon the failure of speech to mediate his alienation and the ultimate inadequacy of embracing the negative role that awaited him as a destructive monster that murderously destroyed in order to see if he could elicit some response from the creator that shunned him. The central tropes of failure parallel those outlined by Frantz Fanon, who also described the dead-end efforts of colonized people to win recognition from those who insisted that they be "Negroes" rather than black and brown women and men whose freedom meant that their lives remained open to their own future acts of self-constitution.

The striking eloquence of Shelley's creature, his gravity and grace (in spite of his huge physical size), are, however, suddenly interrupted in the twentieth century by inchoate groans, by what, in chapter four, we explore as the muting of divine warnings that surrounded efforts to buttress the ultimately illegitimate foundations of modern nations established through genocide, colonialism, and enslavement. For the monster to speak truthfully under such circumstances would enshroud such listeners in a cloak of shame. People belonging to the category of the colonized had nothing to say that those who participated in the discourse of public life wished to hear, especially since the rightfulness of their subordinate membership was supposedly evident in their lack of the ultimate sign of civilization, reason made manifest through language. And yet silence itself is unsettling and ultimately insufficient to appease colonizers. There was, we argue, a further need to hear from the monster affirmations of the world that created him.

After an intermediary period of quiet, the articulate creature reemerged in the last decade of the previous century. He, she, or it speaks over and against the larger category or community of monsters to which he, she, or it, at least in part, belongs. We suggest that such figures are hybrids—some literally belonging to many communities by blood, but many others simply by asymmetrical allegiances. Such hybrid-speaking monsters are asked regularly to articulate their fidelity through making their own monstrous qualities or ties palatable. Such hybrid monsters are, as we will show, a distinguished lot, ranging from Booker T. Washington in the United States at the dawn of the twentieth century, to Nelson Mandela in South Africa during its last decade, to President Barack Obama in the new century. Part of their emergence is linked to another shift at the level of popular culture, a growing desire for and to be like those considered monsters or, we will sometimes qualify, once-monsters. Although this might at first seem like an effort to heed the warnings offered by those who belong to this category, we suggest that it is instead a manifestation of a desire again to avoid both responsibility and judgment by framing oneself, even if only temporarily and at the level of play, as one of the society's victims; it is, in other words, a self-absolving of responsibility through the mystification of self-identity.

Places where disasters strike have a name, "disaster areas," places left, as it were, in ruins. Some of these are sites of efforts to create eternal institutions, monuments that would last forever. Some, not nearly as grand, are the traces of once human communities trounced by unanticipated or terribly handled natural disasters or by sudden and dramatic climatic shifts. There are also the remains of communities that have sought life elsewhere either out of urgent need or simply exhaustion. All ruins are records of human projects that have been abandoned or forcefully interrupted. To walk among them is to remember both that it is we who construct social worlds and that all such efforts come to an end. The ruining of cultures that, for their practitioners, is the end of the world might lack the overt, outward signs of decay. Still, the process forces those committed to preserving antagonized ways of life into tension with subsequent generations. Young people inherit the responsibility for ongoing cultural practices, even if, at times, this demands that they sacrifice the meaning of coming of age—the moment, in their own terms, to try to set the world right. Moreover, the numerous debts accruing by this present generation of adults will demand that our descendants take on the economic bill and other burdens. They in effect will parent their parents. The exhaustion at the very idea of a future lurks, signaling the ways in which failures of this generation to take responsibility in the face of divine warnings endangers the very coherence of a future. It is not until we see what might bring much despair in its wake, as a moment that requires us to think, decide, and act, that we treat disasters as we should—as signs and warnings, as useful, if sobering mirrors whose reflections can enable us maturely to take the weight of forging a tomorrow squarely upon our shoulders.

The difficulty with both disasters and monsters is that it is not always clear what they signify. Even when we are ready to respond, it is not immediately apparent that we will act in ways that eradicate their cause or that do not themselves create new monsters. Still, to create the conditions for dawn rather than simply another day is to aim to achieve healthy continuity, continuity in which we move forward but not forever in the shadows of prior regrettable action. Looking up at the receding stars, after all, we often forget that the rising sun brings with it the casting of new shadows.

◊

1

Signs

We begin with a phenomenon that, in ancient times, fell from the sky. The word *disaster* is astrological in origin. Through a Middle French transformation of the Italian term *disastro,* which means "ill-starred" or "bad-planet," it in turn has origins in Latin (*astrum*) and still earlier in ancient Greek (*astron*). The picture becomes one of an event from which a warning was issued from the heavens, or more precisely, the planets and the stars. Paying close attention to one's astrological charts, it would seem, offers no less than an attunement to the possibility of avoiding, or at least preparing for, bad events or ruin.

How, we may ask, do the stars warn us of such events?

"The queen of the divinatory arts is astrology," writes Richard Cavendish, "which in the Roman world was called *mathesis,* 'the learning,' the pre-eminent branch of knowledge. It owes its prestige to the awe which the starry sky inspires and to the fact that the indicators it uses, the planets and stars, behave in an orderly and predictable way."[1] The configuraton of the stars stands as an occurrence of its own, so with this in mind, we see an event whose signification is another event; it is, in other words, as a sign, a sign deferred and differing, in the sense of being unequal to or at least other than that which it signifies. But since the sign and its signification stand as a continuum of ill-fated events, its appearance is, from the outset, bad.

The events that follow such signs tend to overshadow the signs themselves. Those consequences, which we now know as disasters, are significant in their own right. They are bad things, terrible things, that we wish could have been avoided. And yet "natural disasters" are not naturally disastrous. The failure to read signs leads to such misfortune. Were the signs—the tremor in the earth, ripples in the tide, change in the color of gases emanating from a mountain's peak, sudden transformation of the color of the sky, or changes in wind patterns from an approaching storm; or perhaps animals running to high ground or insects fleeing *en masse*—read properly, perhaps natural phenomena such as earthquakes, tsunamis, volcanic eruptions, tornados, and hurricanes would occur without loss of life, or at least human life. There were, for instance, indigenous people, such as the Moken of the south Pacific and the Indian Ocean, and most certainly animals, who escaped the deadly tsunami in December 2004 because they recognized and heeded the signs that something very dangerous and unusual was rushing onto their shores. They took necessary precautions. These could not have forestalled the devastation to buildings on the coastlines, but they did save lives. In many ways the decision to develop properties so close to the shoreline embodies a refusal to heed the concomitant responsibility to remain vigilant and read signs. The unfortunate reality of the 2008 earthquakes in China revealed the dangers of ignoring the vulnerability of dense populations of people in rapidly and inadequately built facilities across fault lines.

The failure to heed warnings, to read signs properly, is catastrophic. From the ancient Greek word *katastrephein* (which literally means to turn downward or to take a downward turn), the significance of such failure is embodied in its consequence; in catastrophes, we are pushed downward, we, in effect, fall.[2]

To be pushed downward is to face limited options, but in this instance those limits are our own response to crisis—a decision not to act in the face of necessity. The call to act implies the prelogical conjunction of fate and agency. As Richard Cavendish explains, "[I]t was accepted in the ancient world that events cast their shadows before them. All sorts of occurrences were omens of the will of the gods and the trend of the future, generally not as signs of what was bound to happen but of what was likely to happen. A good omen was an encouragement and inspired confidence. A bad omen [such as a fallen star] might be a sign that the gods did not favour a project, a warning of danger in the offing or a signal that the right relationship between gods and men had been disturbed."[3]

Catastrophes could also become disasters, which means that they, too, may stand in a continuum of warnings. To be caught in their field is to face being swallowed up in the avalanche of ill-fated signs. One hopes that the spillage ends at a distance, and, if one is lucky, without having been borne by one's senses, especially that of sight: Not being seen, it cannot be read, and cannot, then, emerge as a sign. To look is to become involved. By covering one's eyes, by looking elsewhere, locking one's doors, seeking the sanctuary of hallowed ground, or even crawling into a hole, one would be passed over and thus lose significance in such a perilous stream. This is not to ignore the significance of the other senses. A tremor, for example, is felt and can occasion shuddering, retraction of the hand, or jumping from the point at which it makes itself known.

The victim of a disaster, one who did see or feel and was thereby enveloped in the continuum, becomes, thus, a marked being. Cavendish writes of efforts to anticipate omens in the signs suggested by corporeal design, "A person's physical peculiarities, mannerisms of speech and walk, the color of his hair, the shape of his nails and the positions of moles on his body were regarded as indications of his character and probable future."[4] In some cases, interpretations of features of birth were insufficient. Enslaved people were branded in the United States, and Jews, gypsies, communists, blacks, and homosexuals interned in Holocaust concentration camps were tattooed. In Europe, North America, South America, and Australia, racism often focused on color as the "mark" that sustained the grammar of branding. Here, we see a move from the technological imposition of demarcation to the logic of the curse, of damnation.[5] Whoever approaches with wounds from an event understood as a disaster or from a life of ill-fatedness stimulates the question, *Is she or he part of its continuum?* Is such an individual also a sign, a fallen star in whose situation the suffering of others has been placed, as is the case of the scapegoat? And what about the witness? Is that person, by coming upon the scene, a custodian and hence a carrier of the message, a divine warning?

There are several responses to these possibilities. The first is to take the notion of a divine warning seriously and, in so doing, take the victim, the survivor, who could also be a victim by virtue of the memory and scars carried, or the witness of disaster, to be a kind of monster. The etymology of "monster" makes this obvious. Derived from the Latin word *monstrum*, which in turn is from the verb *monere*, meaning "to warn or to admonish," it was known as a warning from G-d or the gods. The connection with disaster should be quite obvious, since stars and planets, as thought of over the ages, are in the heavens; they are, in other words, heavenly bodies. Their descent is thus always momentous. A warning suggests that there is something one could do. By doing such, it stimulates a crisis (from the Greek *krenein*, which means "to choose"); it summons choices to be made. Since the results of making the wrong choices could be catastrophic, these kinds of divine warning occasion not only anxiety, the struggle with choices one must make, but also *fear.* The initial sign, then, warns of the catastrophe, but the disaster produces victims who are a continuation of the initial sign; they, in effect, become signs, carrying, like plague, disaster wherever they go. They become, in other words, monsters.[6]

Monsters of disaster are special kinds of divine warning. They are harbingers of things we do not want to face, of catastrophes, and we fear that they will bring such events upon us by coming to us. So, many of us blame such victims. We, by whom we mean simply "we fellow human beings," transform them from effect into cause. They become both the signifier and the signified; their ill fate must, in some way, be of their own doing—their failure properly to have read the signs. *Our* success in reading such signs must, then, take the form of eschewing its messenger.[7] That ability reinforces the view that it must have been an initial failure on the part of the victim of disaster that led to his or her being caught up in the web of disastrous significations, of becoming a warning. "Yes," we are in effect declaring, "we can read the sign," when we blame and abandon such a victim.

This is not to suggest that avoiding contact with specific individuals does not in some instances constitute the reading of signs for which we are arguing. In Camus's *The Stranger,* the reader senses this from the moment Raymond walks through the apartment door of his neighbor Meursault who, facing the death of his mother, agrees to assist Raymond with his romantic woes and becomes embroiled in a tide leading to Meursault committing homicide, being imprisoned, and facing execution.[8] There are disputes and circumstances that we should not enter, for they take on a momentum from which there is no desirable exit. Camus's classic existential novel portrays this phenomenon through suggesting why, in some instances, a character like Meursault may not refuse to become involved and by acting through non-action enters into a sequence of events that buffets him toward what he may not have ordinarily chosen to do but may still have, at least in the vulnerable moments that open the tale, desired. As with Raymond, there are some individuals who, independent of larger forces and events, seem always to appear in the lives of others as a catalyst that initiates a downward spiral of regrettable consequences. Some even seem particularly astute at identifying those who by dint of recent personal matters will be unable to stay outside of battles that they should not take on as their own. The ability of sign continua like Raymond to remain unscathed as they unleash fallout on others is the impetus of countless comic characters from Mr. Bean to Inspector Clouseau. One correctly shudders when they knock at one's door.

There are many historical and recent incidents of victims of disasters who became sign continua, however, through a collective refusal to take responsibility for the conditions that led to their engulfment in catastrophe, from a refusal, in other words, to enter into circumstances and disputes that were properly societal responsibilities. The demonization of the black victims of Hurricane Katrina is a graphic example in recent history.[9] That consequence challenged our ordinary understanding of disaster, since it revealed that not all victims could appear as such. Race was distinguished by two kinds of people in that catastrophe—those who were "innocent" by virtue of being white and those who were already guilty by virtue of being black. The latter's color served as a mark or stain or, in the language of this reading, "sign," that raised the bar of what is required properly to be victims. Timothy Chambers describes this double standard well in his appropriately titled article, "They're Finding Food, but We're Looting?"[10] The discourse, from both right-wing and liberal media, on that event portrayed white (and therefore innocent) victims of a circumstance that was a function of black (and therefore illicit) presence, for the whites did not collapse into the signifier or continuum of the disaster. They became the "we" who faced the "warning," exemplified by the chain of signs from storm to flooding to an overflow of black presence calling for containment. By preserving their whiteness— that is, by not blackening them—the white populations along the Gulf Coastal states struck by the hurricane became the limits of black spillage, the border of monstrous movement. Thus, the constant affirmation of their humanity by the media in the midst of the disaster was also that of black inhumanity, of the danger of an unbound black population.[11] The stories of illicit behavior, of rape and pillage, were themselves the continuum, the movement of signs, that "we" should shun such populations. These representations constructed a projected black state of nature, one that in contrast to an environment governed by whites, who seemed innately to know and honor codes of private property, was barbaric and brutal. Although it would at first seem that white humanity was affirmed in referring to their action with such a phrase as "finding food," we should bear in mind that their closeness to the circumstances also meant that they could be rooted for but not joined; some aspect of the nation's integrity needed to be protected from such disaster spilling over. The whole circumstance must, that is, not be their fault, since what would follow from them, as the proper exemplars of the nation, would also be the nation's culpability. As in all theodicy, where evil is explained as invasive, something from without, such responsibility must come from elsewhere, from the monstrous tide that continued past the borders of the ill-fated city, rather than from a failure of the nation's leadership to develop an adequate political response, as witnessed in recent times not only in the United States but also in Burma/Myanmar.

The people who went to the heart of the disaster were truly courageous souls. Stories await regarding the reach of the disastrous continuum, transformed into continua, of the movement of signs that permeated the nation as the messengers of the event, those whose lives constituted by its message, were absorbed across the nation as harbingers of disaster. The economy and the moral conscience of the nation rippled; political reputations were endangered; and many more aspects of contemporary life were shaken. One might consider here the courageous work of Martin Delaney, the famed black physician, novelist, jurist, and social theorist, who, facing the outbreak of a cholera epidemic in Pittsburgh, Pennsylvania, in 1854, remained while others with equivalent medical training fled, organized a team of male and female nurses, and provided medical care for the city. Recall as well that Michel Foucault's oft-cited discussion of the *panopticon* in *Discipline and Punish* begins with reflections on the situation of the plague. In his view, the image of the plague and plague-struck town "stands for all forms of confusion and disorder." It is within this state of nature that jurists imagine the "utopia of the perfectly governed city," perfect disciplinary functions that separate unpredictable crowds into individuated, organized units.[12] The reference to plague brings to the fore our theme of the signifying continuum, literally the contagion of the meaning of disaster.

One need not look only at the events that followed Katrina and the cyclone in Burma to see how the ascription of divine warning occasions anxiety and fear. There have been social disasters as well, the consequence of which has been a set of people who function as divine warnings. In the United States, for example, the destruction of the public infrastructure for effective schools took a form that is similar to the situations of individuals resisting the warnings to leave New Orleans as the storm approached and the realities they suffered during its onslaught and in its aftermath. Such social devastation was racially conditioned. What else are white schools that seem to "find" the resources they need versus predominantly black and brown schools that have become synonymous with wasted resources and failure? What else are the responses, such as white flight, the very deliberate creation of school zones that isolate students of color and the poor, charter schools with admissions procedures that predetermine who will be able to apply, or the development of internal structures of separation (such as tracking predominantly white college-bound programs) to an influx of black students tipping the low percent ceiling in "good" schools (often less than five but maximally twelve percent black) imposed on them? The result of self-reflection from such black students is the earlier-mentioned collapse of effect into cause: Their failure to read the significance of their racialization, of their being black, delimits their ability to stray. Although the reality here is often that of black *and brown* schools, the nation's anxiety about race creates, to build on a concept from Pierre Bourdieu, a social field of blackness as antipodal to the ideal of whiteness.[13]

For many designated "brown" people, this often means finding a haven in Catholic schools and universities that lack a sufficiently large black population through which to escape, or at least attempt to escape, the American racial continuum. We thus focus on black signification here since it is the primary *sign* of disaster in the country. In countries such as France and Germany, such a continuum is at the moment more brown in the national consciousness because there is not a sufficient concentration of blacks to occasion such fear as in England, but reports of attacks on black students in those countries, as well as in such Asian countries as China and Japan, suggest that in fear of brown is also a fear of a gravitational pull down into blackness.[14] The disaster of the public schools, they fail to see, is *in* them, is exemplified *by* them. This is believed in spite of the obvious contradiction: Blacks perform well in predominantly black countries such as Antigua and Ghana, and even in a country with a large black population and a social commitment to their performance, such as Cuba.[15] A black public school is, in other words, a form of divine warning. Students in such schools do increasingly read the signs. Consider, for example, the reflections of two teenage girls interviewed by Jonathan Kozol about the ongoing project of segregating schools. One reflected, "It's like we're being hidden. It's as if you have been put in a garage where, if they don't have room for something but aren't sure if they should throw it out, they put it there where they don't need to think of it again." Another student commented, "Think of it this way ... If people in New York woke up one day and learned that we were gone, that we had simply died or left for somewhere else, how would they feel? I think they'd be relieved."[16]

In similar kind to Hurricane Katrina, there are brave individuals who devote their lives to such a disaster, who face being drawn into the continuum of signs that constitute its reach. These are people who are willing to risk being swept up in the tide of signification by looking at such signs instead of avoiding them, and by doing so, incurring the wrath of those who have been forced to behold what they did not want to see. These people are, in the end, dangerous people. It is not only black students in such schools who are treated as monsters in our society but also their teachers, whose efforts to stem the waves lead to their being swallowed up by them. While incurring such wrath, many such teachers, however, work within the same semiotic structure because they work in schools to which they would never dream of sending their own children.

Yet there are other portraits that can be made of victims of disaster and the hostility they may face as they reach out for the proverbial kindness of strangers. Instead of becoming a monster, Simone Weil argues that the individual who becomes a divine warning should properly be characterized as *afflicted.* She observes:

> Men have the same carnal nature as animals. If a hen is hurt, the others rush up and peck it. The phenomenon is as automatic as gravitation. Our senses attach to affliction all the contempt, all the revulsion, and all the hatred, which our reason attaches to crime.[17]

An afflicted person suffers a catastrophe; he or she is, in effect, struck down. Weil's definition of "affliction," in this regard, is worth a long quotation:

> Affliction is an uprooting of life, a more or less attenuated equivalent of death, made irresistibly present to the soul by the attack

or immediate apprehension of physical pain. If there is complete absence of physical pain there is no affliction for the soul, because thought can turn itself away in any direction. Thought flies from affliction as promptly and irresistibly as an animal flies from death.... There is no real affliction unless the event, which has gripped and uprooted a life, attacks it, directly or indirectly, in all its parts, social, psychological, and physical. The social factor is essential. There is not really affliction where there is not social degradation or the fear of it in some form or another.... The great enigma of human life is not suffering but affliction.... At the very best, he who is branded by affliction will only keep half his soul.[18]

Weil saw much redemption in affliction. For her, it is, in effect, the immensity of G-d in contact with the hubris of an expanding soul. G-d crushes us through contacting, "touching," us, and in the emptying of the ego that follows from the suffering and humiliation borne by such an encounter, one is left open to G-d. Here, she captures the spirit, so to speak, of worship in theistic societies, where enthusiasm, literally letting G-d or the gods *in*, is its guiding feature.[19] We see here Weil's peculiar twist on theodicy. Instead of blaming the victim for his or her calamities, she affirms the goodness and justness of G-d by congratulating, perhaps even envying, the afflicted. Disaster, suffering signaled from the heavens, is, in this reading, a gift. In a reversal of the theodician logic that we have described, Weil urges readers to attach special value and actively seek out the unique insights and divine access of the despised. Yet poetic and theologically rich though her portrait might be, Weil was wise enough to know that it would occasion very few volunteers.

Portraying the victim of disaster as afflicted explains, to some extent, the courageous souls in a different light. For instead of a divine warning, such people regard the victim of disaster as a divine calling or cry that should ignite that within us which is also good and divine. But the paradox of such a portrait is that it works best if the suffering were not interpreted as affliction. Reaching out to a calling from G-d, pious though it may be, is not the same as risking losing everything in a circumstance that just happened to turn out to be a call from G-d. In other words, for the argument to work, the courageous soul must not know it. And since the reach of the sign of disaster could be continuous, it means, as well, that the victim of disaster must not also know that it is a form of affliction. With stakes so high, is it any wonder that the response, especially among those wrapped in a theodicy in which they prize their good fortune as evidence of their piety, is to look away from the afflicted, to regard such victims, in the end, as bad news?

There is, however, at least a third possibility. Ellen K. Feder has argued in a discussion of physicians' responses to intersex patients that the patients often experience a form of shame from not being curable or being extraordinarily difficult to fix.[20] Fanon observed a similar phenomenon in the treatment of North Africans in France in the early 1950s. As he reflected:

> Medical thinking proceeds from the symptom to the lesion. In the illustrious assemblies, in the international medical congresses, agreement has been reached as to the importance of the neurovegetative systems, the diencephalons, the endocrine glands, the psychosomatic links, the sympathalgias, but doctors continue to be taught that every symptom requires its lesion. The patient, who complains of headaches, ringing in his ears, and dizziness, will also have high blood pressure. But should it happen that along with these symptoms there is no sign of high blood-pressure, nor of brain tumor, in any case nothing positive, the doctor would have to conclude that medical thinking was at fault; and as any thinking is necessarily thinking about something, he will find the *patient* at fault—an indocile, undisciplined patient, who doesn't know the rules of the game.[21]

The physician's frustration at the patient for not being a good patient, here defined as one whose body facilitates being cured, also leads to shame on the part of the patient. The patient suffers the shame of having done something wrong, namely, of disappointing the physician. The intersexed patient suffers from straining fixed norms; the North African "who goes to see a doctor bears the dead weight of all his compatriots."[22] Shame, however, has a dual structure here, for it is the physician's frustration that at times places the physician before him or herself in the form of a failed effort, which, as Sara Ahmed observes, "feels like an exposure—another sees what I have done that is bad and hence shameful—but it also involves an attempt to hide, a hiding that requires the subject turn away from the other and towards itself."[23] The subterranean shame experienced by the physician is, however, not at first a function of epistemological impotence in the face of the patient, whose structural relation is of an inferior since the intersexed and the North African patients in Feder's and Fanon's discussions are not at the normative center embodied by the physician. The physician's shame occurs through another site of projected ideality. As Ahmed explains: "In shame, I expose to myself that I am a failure through the gaze of an ideal other."[24] A deterioration of relations emerges as the shame of a revealed weakness, including the shame of being ashamed in front of a supposed inferior, leads to acts of concealment, where the patient becomes the harbinger of bad signs.

Feder's and Fanon's insight thus offers a different explanation of the anxiety and fear occasioned by victims of disaster. The sign signified by the victim is our own impotence. In our not being able to erase the disaster, we become frustrated at those who failed to have read its signs: Why didn't they leave? Why did they choose to live there? Why did they choose to live in trailer parks or makeshift shacks in areas known for natural disasters? Why? Why? Why? What was wrong with *them*?

Such views erase the distinction between choice and option. One's choices cannot transform the options available. They could only affect how we relate to those options. To address options, one must go beyond oneself to the world that constitutes them. There are options from nature, such as our biological makeup and the chemical or physical components of our pre-social environment. And then there are those that are a function of the human world and its concomitant social world. That world affects our options by endowing them with meanings that are broader than each individual; it impacts, as well, the environment by transforming it into a chain of signification that we may call "cultural." In this sense, options carry with them responsibility. Here, a disaster can be read as a circumstance or circumstances in which, regardless of intentions, options are so limited that intense suffering and even ruin are the result. Here, the source of frustration and desire to blame the victim of disaster is a consequence of a subterranean truth: "society, unlike biochemical processes, cannot escape human influences. Man is what brings society into being."[25]

Disasters, although revealing our impotence, emphasize the need for our agency, for a political response. Much early twenty-first-century obsession with disaster is symptomatic of anxiety of the political right over the need for politics and political institutions. This manifests itself in multiple ways, including the search for privatized solutions to public problems or for religious-based aid agencies to replace the need for government services. One sees this as well on the political left, which continue to defend politics through being discursive, but often fail actually to develop viable answers to the question of what is to be done. Many within these ranks also turn to valorize the work of local NGOs, their own counterparts to the privatized charity models advocated by conservatives. These agencies, from the standpoint of the left, are to stimulate the kind of active grassroots participation that might lead to a revived public and political life, and yet, more immediately, signal a deep impotence. A clear indication of this is the rise of moralistic reasoning and moralizing in both instances. The left write moralistic appeals against the failures of the right to respond to the disaster; the right simply blame the left for the social conditions that maintained an environment of susceptible people. The left respond that vulnerability to disaster is a function of social options. The right counter that there are limits to who should be responsible for other people's social welfare and on whose lives are most deserving of such responsibility.

Moralizing simplifies and stabilizes a complex world in flux and allows us to put at a distance what might otherwise be too near. Moralizing turns on de- and a-contextual thinking in which people or circumstances alone are reductionistically blamed for what is always a complex mediation of both. Examples of this abound: an obsession with car seats and with fining parents who fail to use them while not putting in place the conditions for their availability in all vehicles such as cabs, school buses, city buses, trains, and ferries. A bewildering sense that our children are not safe finds seemingly quick solutions in individuals, but not the state, that can be forced to pay. It is a similar situation with, for example, child abuse. There is a generalized sense that the society in which we live is sick, without a coherent understanding of the relationship between adults and children. Rather than a conversation about and the rallying of political resources to develop coherent policies, there is an obsession with the failure of government-related agencies to intervene in child abuse situations, some of which end in violent death. Yet there is an absence of support for what such agencies would need to function as actual havens for children. Our aim is not to diminish the significance of such things as car safety and intervention on behalf of children in dangerous situations. We are here voicing concern about the ways in which these policies direct attention away from larger political questions of social responsibility by collapsing into an individuating and individualistic moralism. Social, cultural, and political problems give way to identifying easy culprits whom we can collectively scorn.

This is not to say that there should be no accounting for individual responsibility. Hannah Arendt reflected in the 1960s in her essay "Personal Responsibility Under Dictatorship," the deep aversion in popular culture to judging and assigning responsibility to individuals, that the very logic on which courts rely, culpable individuals, was resisted deeply at the level of culture.[26] Everyone seemed to say that faced with similarly horrific situations, all would be equally guilty. In lieu of this aversion to judgment she urged that we must engage in such reflection on what is involved in being a thinking person. What thinking people do is ask, "If I were to do that, would I be able to live with myself?" Moralism disguises itself in the clothes of someone willing to undertake the reflection required of judging, but it in fact latches on instead to self-righteous forms of making judgments, to a reflexive ascription of blame, an ongoing failure actually to consider the nature of responsibility.

Judgment requires criteria through which there could be an understanding of the limits of rules. It is no accident that the word *critic* shares etymological roots with criteria, criticism, critique, and crisis—namely, the Greek word *krenein* (to choose), from which the word *krites* (judge) was derived. The realization that choice related to the things needed to make them—criteria, evidence—means that in judgment there is also its limit, that a decision has to be made. Judgmentalism requires a decision prior to criteria; it involves treating some circumstances as a pre-concluded law. To be judgmental, which is not the same as judging, is to refuse fully to engage and read the signs before one by making the accused individual a continuum of the sign. The failure turns on a desire to distance oneself from what is discomforting, to make it impossible that one might be responsible for such an abomination. This is what is so strange about this moment: in our aversion to addressing disasters as signs and our mythopoetic understanding of them as falling stars or monsters as divine warnings, we actively create monsters and enemies and thereby maintain moments of hysteria, refusing actually to interpret and take responsibility for the kinds of collective response that may be needed to alleviate human misery.

Responding requires genuine thinking and acting, both of which refer to a set of principles to which one might appeal. Consider these reflections of Ortega y Gasset, which we quote at length:

> An idea is putting a truth in checkmate. Whoever wishes to have ideas must first prepare himself to desire truth and to accept the

rules of the game imposed by it. It is no use speaking of ideas when there is no acceptance of authority to regulate them, a series of standards to which it is possible to appeal in discussion. These standards are the principles on which culture rests. I am not concerned with the form they take. What I affirm is that there is no culture where there are no standards to which our fellow-men can have recourse. There is no culture where there are no principles of legality to which to appeal. There is no culture where there is no acceptance of certain final intellectual positions to which the dispute may be referred.... When all these things are lacking there is no culture; there is in the strictest sense of the word, barbarism ... The average man finds himself with "ideas" in his head, but he lacks the faculty of ideation. He has no conception even of the rare atmosphere in which ideas live. He wishes to have opinions, but is unwilling to accept the conditions and presuppositions that underlie all opinion. Hence his ideas are in effect nothing more than appetites in words.... To have an idea means believing one is in possession of the reasons for having it, and consequently means believing that there is such thing as reason, a world of intelligible truths. To have ideas, to form opinions, is identical with appealing to such an authority, submitting oneself to it, accepting its code and its decisions, and therefore believing that the highest form of intercommunion is the dialogue in which the reasons for our ideas are discussed.[27]

Gasset, for his part, a Spanish parliamentarian and philosopher, was impressed by the principles of liberalism, which he argued represented "the loftiest endeavor towards common life." It could be nothing short of a supreme form of generosity that majorities within it conceded rights to minorities, thereby "announc[ing] determination to share existence with an enemy; more than that, with an enemy which is weak."[28] He noted that this "noble," "refined," and "acrobatic" attitude was also "anti-natural" and that it was not surprising that "this same humanity would soon appear anxious to get rid of it." It required a "discipline too difficult and complex to take root from the earth."[29]

The contrast between this attitude and that of the German legal theorist Carl Schmitt, who wrote in the same period, could not be starker. He stressed the indispensability of enemies to political life, but charged advocates of liberalism with downplaying the difficulties of incorporating and coexisting with them to its detriment.[30] Liberals, he claimed, proceeded as if all matters could be dealt with through negotiation. If this proved limited, then such questions were simply deferred. Not everything, Schmitt argued, could be reduced to the frameworks of economics and debate. There were, he insisted, differences that could not be mediated: could democracies, for instance, coherently tolerate antidemocratic parties? What of communities that aimed to subordinate the power of other collectivities? For Schmitt, the political emerged in moments when any group that could mobilize citizens around its designation of shared friends and enemies did so, sharpening a sense of the substance of its own political identity and the kinds of exclusions required to sustain it. The political therefore emerged in the identification of moments in which the rule of law and established political procedures could not apply.[31]

After a period in which most political and social theorists, especially those in North America, thought it appropriate to ignore Schmitt's writings, especially because of his involvement with the Nazi Party, many others have recently been drawn to this work, which shares many sympathies with postmodern writers who have framed the effort to create collective identities and hegemonic political programs as totalizing acts of domination. Within both are aversions to the mediation and active compromise at the core of political life. In Schmitt, this takes the form of a desire for a powerful dictatorial leader who will act (with our acclaim) as godlike and be immune to the criticisms and procedural interventions of others. Schmitt emphasized that his work was not a call for ongoing war or militarization. Yet his stressing moments of exception in which someone emerges as sovereign by identifying collective friends and enemies emphasizes the political as the point at which group differences cannot be mediated diplomatically. To compromise, in such circumstances, is to jeopardize the substance of one's group identity. Such logic lends itself easily to a political climate in which we can spend massively on the industry of war while we scorn the idea of investing in constructive politics or developing our infrastructure, because, it has been claimed, as the attacks on social programs over the past two-and-a-half decades aver, these mechanisms are broken. Would such declaration of things being broken lead to the financial infusions that come as they do for the military when wars show no immediate sign of offering victory, the nation could probably find itself close to the once-longed-for Age of Aquarius.[32] Our point here is not to attack Schmitt so much as an effort to interpret his widespread academic appeal as a sign, to read the significance of such attraction to a theoretical account of the impossibility of liberal democracies as we know them.

The calamity of broken government is profitable for some. Naomi Klein, for example, contends:

> Call it disaster capitalism. Every time a new crisis hits—even when the crisis is itself the direct by-product of free market ideology— the fear and disorientation that follow are harnessed for radical social and economic re-engineering. Each new shock is midwife to a new course of economic shock therapy. The end result is the same kind of unapologetic partition between the included and the excluded, the protected and the damned, that is on display in Baghdad.[33]

Immediately following sudden infrastructural breakdowns are calls for private investors to compete with one another to see which offers the best, deregulated fix. The preferred responses to disasters do not treat them as exceptional moments that require pulling together over and against abiding, atomizing differences. Instead "recovery" consists in measures that further polarize the people and places they claim to mend: some are simply left to their own devices surrounded by wreckage while others "ascend to a parallel privatized state, one equipped with well-paved highways and skyways, safe bridges, boutique charter schools, fast-lane airport terminals, and deluxe subways."[34] These are symptoms, argues Klein, of a transition from a military-industrial-complex to a fast growing disaster-capitalism-complex. The latter employs corporations to fight wars and police borders, to treat traumatized soldiers and to construct schools. One such company in the U.S. South offers to book luxury holidays as warnings of coming storms approach, transforming what would be an evacuation into "a jet-setter vacation."

Klein emphasizes that where disaster capitalism takes root, there is always a proliferation of non-state armed groups. She writes, "That is hardly a surprise: when countries are rebuilt by people who don't believe in governments, the states they build are invariably weak, creating a market for alternative security forces, whether Hezbollah, Blackwater, the Mahdi Army, or the gang down the street in New Orleans."[35] These states within states, built with public resources and often staffed by former government employees, are as powerful as the formal ones are weak, yet significantly, they cannot be held to account. This is especially significant since many such corporations are avowedly partisan.

The disturbing consequence of these trends is that the state, especially in the United States in the first decade of the new millennium, has actually broken. Its equipment is relatively outmoded and its most talented people regularly leave it for the private sector on which the government has relied. This pattern led Thomas Frank, in *Wrecking Crew*, to insist that the crumbling and decimation associated with the administration of George W. Bush was not the anomaly that many conservative Republicans preferred to claim. Instead, Frank demonstrates, it was the inevitable result of an antigovernment approach to governing, one that aimed to prove the inherent weakness of government by ensuring that it failed to work constructively and then proceeding to sell off "big government" through deregulation, underfunding, and the process of public policy making as a private-sector bidding war. Frank warns that "deliberate misgovernment" cannot be reversed primarily or only through standard electoral remedies. Having created disaster-complex markets, these are now terrains to be guarded. Many disaster-related corporations regard the state and nonprofits as competitors, arguing that if people had reason to expect that the government would protect them, there would be no incentive to pay for their services.

One consequence of all of this is that what once functioned as a truism, that bad political times were also bad for the economy, no longer seems to be true. Global instability is translating into massive profits for those in heavy construction, private healthcare, oil and gas sectors, and defense contractors to the point that "many people around the world have come to the same conclusion: the rich and powerful must be deliberately causing the catastrophes so that they can exploit them."[36] Klein insists that these are not the secret dark hatchings of conspiracies but instead the inevitable outcome of an economic system that requires constant growth, resists any environmental regulation, and seeks short-term profits and dirty energy sources. Unless we displace these as governing norms, the fallout and the profits generated by it will continue. Klein concludes, "Disaster generation can therefore be left to the market's invisible hand. This is one area in which it actually delivers."[37]

Kenneth Saltman, drawing on the work of Klein and David Harvey, demonstrates that although making business opportunities out of public schools is not new, and that there are now many publicly recorded and widely known instances of failures following the privatization of schools, a different strategy, what Saltman calls "back door" or "smash and grab" privatization, has emerged. Focusing on the examples of the educational rebuilding of New Orleans and Iraq, Saltman documents how for-profit educational contractors moved into these places, framing their work as the "silver lining" and "golden opportunities" of these disasters. Eschewing public control and oversight as unnecessarily cumbersome and wasteful, their own record is actually of failure at the avowed aim while being consistently successful at redistributing wealth upward. Building on Harvey, Saltman argues that the process of taking publicly owned goods and transforming them into private, restricted ones is "the continuation of 'enclosing the commons' begun in Tudor England."[38] Surely, Saltman rhetorically queries, pillaging public schools for profit interrupts one of their historic functions of reproducing class relations, preparing a small set of managers and a large, docile workforce? The students in schools that are wrecked and rebuilt for profit, answers Saltman, are already presumed to be disposable. They are not being prepared as workers because no work awaits them. They are instead, as Jean Anyon has argued, "learning to do time," being prepared for the next big punitive industry for which their bodies represent nothing more than commodities.

In our portrait of liberal to left interventions on the one hand and conservative to right-wing ones on the other, we see an asymmetrical situation that is often posed as a symmetrical one in a logic of both sides. The reason they are not symmetrical is that they have entirely opposed aims. For the liberal-through-left approach, the project relies on discursive practices, the very essence of which requires opposition. The conservative-to-right-wing approach is primarily interested in order and rule. Such an objective can be gained *at the expense* of eliminating all oppositions. Since even one's opponent must be provided a place in the former, there is an implicit egalitarian consequence. Since one's opponent must be eliminated in the latter, the logical conclusion is, in a word, fascism. The consequences are seen today in the distinction between neoliberalism and neoconservatism. Although the free market functions as the theology of both, the former would like the preservation of civil liberties whereas the latter—as The War on Terror, marked by torture, unconstrained surveillance, and the rise of a sham press on the right reveal—are willing to discard them.

Disasters demand, as we have been arguing, community responses. A radically individualistic ethics and politics leave little room for such an option. And more, the need for social infrastructures that would enable natural phenomena simply to be such, edifices that could assure that the consequences of an unexpected calamity are, in a word, contained, where the sign continuum is limited, is anathema in a world governed by rule over politics. Where rule is primary, containment does not focus on minimizing the impact of a calamity but on transforming its spillage into order. Thus, law enforcement and military intervention receive support—all of which are, in fact, even where purportedly privatized and often left to the creative force of the illicit economy, government-supported activity—over things that could have avoided chaos in the first place, such as good levees (New Orleans), accessible health care (the sign continuum of diseases that becomes pandemics), employment (poverty and crime), and appropriately supported education systems (illiteracy, poverty, and crime). Accompanying such displacement is, as Jean Comaroff and John Comaroff have argued, a fetishism of judiciary or legalistic activities effecting disorder and a rise in social misery. "Everywhere these days, criminal violence has become an imaginative vehicle, a hieroglyph almost, for thinking about the nightmares that threaten the nation and for posing 'more law and order' as the appropriate means of dealing with them. And everywhere the discourse of crime displaces attention away from the material and social effects of neoliberalism, blaming its darker undersides on the evils of the underworld."[39]

The cynicism about the ability to affect the world positively through politics, to address the conditions suggested by disaster so as to forestall the negative impact of future disasters, is also evident in the attack on all forms of noninstructional teaching and learning, anything which instead of showing immediately measurable results might ask instead what is worth measuring. The rationalization for this turn took for granted the failure of public education programs of the late 1960s through the 1970s, even though the actual data do not support such a conclusion. Investing in better public schools, especially in the inner cities, did lead to a rise in high school graduates, students entering colleges, and students entering graduate schools in the 1970s into the 1980s.[40] Still, even the most instrumental of education suggests a world in which one might engage or more minimally to which one might adjust, one with a mundane social fabric that one might strengthen or refashion. A genuine education for emergency or for perpetual disaster would require the cultivation of practical reason, good judgment, and the ability to think and act where contingency is the rule. Even in such circumstances, questions of value cannot be avoided, even though a criticism of liberal education has been that it lacks a treatment of values. Such a criticism often conceals its real complaint, which is not about values but about *which values.*

Much talk of public education in countries dominated by neoliberalism and neoconservatism is saturated with the language of crisis. Proponents of the right have orchestrated this crisis through an assault on public places and the advancement of a set of narrow skills over and against the very notion of education as a preparation for civic life. Many on the left have, by moving away from fighting for state responsibility and waging a fight against hegemony and the articulating of standards, abrogated their role as defenders of public life and politics. Our education systems, with few exceptions, do not prepare us for disasters, because we are interested in manufacturing and continuing, rather than reading or learning from such phenomena. Remaining in crises, standing paralyzed, in the face of disaster, cannot be the *telos,* the aim, of education. The word "education" is derived, we should remember, from the Latin word *educare,* which means "to raise" or "to bring up" and a cognate of *educere* or "to lead out." What more fitting a response could there be to what we have been calling the sign-continuum of disaster than to learn how to go beyond it?

The neoconservative and neoliberal epoch is, however, distinguished, among other things, by a neurotic fear of reality. It is as though reality itself has become the sign continuum, that is, a disaster. It is no accident that some of the most spacious political conversation in contemporary life takes place on comedy shows. To be funny, humor requires a kernel of accuracy that is not possible when one is thinking or talking dogmatically. If aimed at the already converted, it evokes a moment of catharsis as a blow is struck against the often-feared government officials and their policies. The laughter it evokes is also more ritualistic. Genuine humor forces us into proximity and distance with our own positions and those of others, inviting us to reflect on the inconvenient truths and images of all positions. Humor, in this way, is uniquely pedagogical; it allows us safely to try on other roles and ideas that can open the way to the rules of genuine thinking and persuasion described by Ortega y Gasset.

But humor also has its limitations. Fanon, for instance, related the importance of humor whose cultivation was worth developing even by identifying his enemies and making a scene.[41] Humor offered him a naive view on the discursive, where he sought simply the reaching of others through the force of truth and argumentation; but, as he admitted, he had to change his tune since even reason took flight from him (the sign continuum), which led to his descent into Negritude, an ideology of black superiority, in his effort to subvert the catastrophe through its affirmation. That moment of solace was, however, struck by a divine warning, as Fanon acknowledged, through Jean-Paul Sartre's essay, "Black Orpheus," in which Negritude was shown to be an effort to escape reality, a looking away from it.[42] Fanon lamented: "Yesterday, awakening to the world, I saw the sky turn upon itself utterly and wholly. I wanted to rise, but the disemboweled silence fell back upon me, its wings paralyzed. Without responsibility, straddling Nothingness and Infinity, I began to weep."[43]

After crying, Fanon was able to face reality, which was the theme of his next chapter of *Black Skin, White Masks*, "Psychopathology and the Negro," in which he argued that the modern world has no coherent notion of what it means to be a healthy black adult. The text is an exploration of the many efforts at responding to these problems without recourse to their social genesis. Our point about the need for social responses is, in other words, not a new one.

We are not responsible for a rock suddenly falling out of the sky. But we are responsible for the social conditions by which that rock could be transformed into a disaster. And as our technology increases our ability to predict the movement of natural phenomena, it also brings along with it the responsibility for the kind of damage that can be unleashed by such things on the world of the living.

The portraits we have offered here are different perspectives on a single phenomenon. In disasters, whose sibling is catastrophe, there is a striking down of individuals in ways that suggest condemnation. Here, we move to the realm of the damned, whose etymological roots point to the Latin *damnum*, which refers to loss or hurt or, as in the obvious cognate, "damage." It is no accident that the fear and anxiety about recent disasters relate to their signification of an impending spillover of populations whose options are reduced daily in this age of neoliberal globalism of market forces and neoconservative demands for forceful world order, the consequence of which has been a growing disorder.[44]

We find ourselves now reflecting on what Frantz Fanon called the condemned or damned of the earth. Here, we bear witness to people who live under limited options wrought by a calamity that historically fell upon them as if from out of the sky. The disaster of colonialism and racism has been the creation of disastrous subjects, of people who are marked as the continued sign of ill fate and ruin. These people, whom W.E.B. Du Bois more than a century ago also identified as "problem people," are sites of damnation.[45] This is not to say that there are not among them those who "rise." It is that their ascent does not function in the same way as those in groups without the significance of disaster. With the latter, the project of rising becomes the rule instead of the exception. The logic of condemnation means that such achievement is more the exception than the rule with the implication that one cannot rise as a member of *that* group. Think about the adage of being "damned if you do, damned if you don't."

The conscience of society is such, however, that it offers little room for survivors of what should not have gone out of control. We have explored how such survivors stimulate fear and trembling. It is not only that they have survived, but also that they pose, in their survival, the challenge to others of surviving *them*. That is why, as Elias Canetti observed, survivors are often destroyed, especially by despots.[46] The continuation of a survivor means, in effect, that others must die. Better him or her than the rest of us. In other words, *we* must become survivors. How, we may ask, then, do imperial societies articulate survival? It is through the affirmation of the value of one set of lives over others, a value that could only be confirmed through the unleashing of death. In the language we have been using, that means pushing the sign-continuum into another direction. In the death of every Iraqi is, proleptically, the survival of every American; the death of Natives, the survival of settlers; the death of Palestinians, the survival of Israel; the death of Israel, the survival of Palestine; the death of gays, the survival of heterosexuals; the death of blacks, the survival of whites; the death of Africans, the affirmation of life for the rest of the world.

Fanon ended nearly all of his books with reflections on how important it is for communities to learn how to move on, to look at the horizon of a star-filled sky at dawn's door. The consequence of such is his often-misunderstood notion of setting afoot a new humanity. We hope that our explorations have shown that taking flight is, in effect, an effort to avoid a situation the result of which is its continuation. To move on requires the affirming embrace of the human being within us through the affirmation of social reality itself, of the *yes* that is of, if not a courageous soul, at least a sober one in the world of others.

◇

2

Warnings

Our discussion of disaster identified a variety of divine warnings. As we saw, the monster, or at least the tendency to create monsters, is one manifestation. The etymology of the word "monster," as we have already seen, points to the Latin word *monstrum*, which means warning. That word in turn emerges from the verb *monere*, to warn or to admonish, and its relation to the word "demonstrate" reminds us that it also means to show. So right away, we know that where there are monsters, something has gone wrong. The monster is, in effect, a sign, which, in premodern times, was summoned from G-d or the gods. Such warnings were thus also of divine significance. There is, then, a lesson to be learned from such creatures; they speak to us, summoning in us a crisis of the self, because it is we who are being warned, which means that there must be something *we* are ultimately doing wrong and that it is up to *us* to fix. Monsters, then, alert us to choices we need to make, and where there are choices, there is also, in addition to fear and trembling, as existential philosophers remind us, anxiety.[1]

A basic feature of monsters is that they exemplify exaggeration or extremes, which, in the scheme of ancient worldviews, illustrated well in Aristotelian thought, always signifies a fall from virtue. The Aristotelian notion also lends itself to the etymology of monsters, even though his ancient Greek philosophical analysis precedes the emergence of the term in the Latin world, since the divine or the blessed, as translations of *eudaimonia*, that at which the good man's actions are aimed, works in his schema as a teleological model of reality itself.[2] With regard to all of reality, in Aristotle's view, all natural things have a purpose and are technically not bad except through a deviation from its nature. Thus, a divine warning could only emerge from deviation from

29

either a natural functioning or, in the world of human actions, the model of a balanced life.

We thus already encounter a precondition for monsters, namely, that they require a normative naturalism. We say "normative" for two reasons. First, in the old, teleological models of nature, the normative and the natural converged. To function naturally meant to do so in the right way. The second reason is that the term *natural* is already loaded with normative content well into the present. The ascription of being monstrous is a value placed upon a thing which surfaces as the "unnatural" or the "hypernatural." This does not, however, mean that monstrosity must be conditioned by the dictates of modern scientific naturalism. We should bear in mind that naturalism need not be incompatible with spiritualism nor the theological worldviews that succeeded Aristotle's in the Middle Ages, since even spiritualists and deists have the notion of a natural kind, even within the sphere of the spiritual itself. One could imagine, for example, the notion of an unnatural spirit, as some religions such as Christianity and Islam aver, in which there are devils or demons and other kinds of evil beings challenging forces of good in the world. But more germane to the history of the concept, the link between the natural and the normative emerges through what it means for there to be a standard. A natural kind is that which meets the standard. Thus, returning to spirituality, deism, and notions of divine warning, the gods or G-d would be considered the source of natural standards the deviation from which constitutes the "unnatural." In this sense, at least from the point of view of Christianity and Islam, all monsters are unnatural or they, as suggested at the outset, alert us to something we are doing that is unnatural. From the standpoint of Judaism, however, there was a different interpretation that occasioned much difficulty for Jews in the Christian world. As Richard Cavendish reports in the Christian context:

> The Devil never bulked as large in Judaism as in Christianity and the demons [which Jews believed existed], though dangerous and frightening, had all been created by God himself and were part of the divine scheme of things. There was not the same deep horror of trafficking with them as in Christianity, in which they were dedicated enemies of the faith. Magic posed no threat to religion and society, and there were no persecutions of sorcerers and witches remotely comparable to the holocausts of witches in Christian Europe. On the other hand, the more relaxed Jewish attitude to magic and demons may have contributed to Christian persecution of the Jews,

by reinforcing the belief that all Jews were demon-worshippers and sorcerers.... In Christian eyes [in the Middle Ages] the Jews were the children and servants of Satan, who had incited them to crucify Christ. They were suspected of poisoning wells and spreading epidemics, torturing wax images of Jesus, stabbing consecrated hosts, crucifying Christian children and using their blood in the Passover service (a Russian Jew was tried on this charge as late as 1913). Allegations of sorcery, not so much against individual Jews as *en masse*, were a frequent prelude to massacres. The wicked Jew, shaggy, bearded, horned, filthy, stinking and skilled in evil magic—like Satan—was a stock figure of Christian folk belief. Attempts were made to force all Jews to wear horned hats as a mark of their diabolic allegiance. They were rumoured to worship the Evil One in the form of a cat or a toad in their synagogues, where they invoked his help in their malevolent designs. Many of the accusations made against them were also brought against Christian heretics and witches, and the terms 'synagogue' and 'sabbath' were taken over from Judaism and applied to the meetings of witches.[3]

Christendom in the Middle Ages also offered a pairing of Jews and Muslims, especially in its western shores in the form of the Moors. The Moors were North African Muslims who had conquered the Iberian Peninsula and much of the Mediterranean in the eighth century and ruled that region till their defeat in Grenada in the fifteenth century.[4] Jews and Moors came together in the emergence of the word *raza*, which, according to Sebastian de Covarrubias in 1611, referred to "the caste of purebred horses, which are marked by a brand so that they can be recognized ... Raza in lineages is meant negatively, as in having some raza of Moor or Jew."[5] That the etymology of the word *race* is from *raza* exemplifies the normative course from theological naturalism to its modern form as documented in Francois Bernier's "A New Division of the Earth."[6]

We already see that some naturalisms work through a teleological or directed order, which means that deviation in such instances is tantamount to going against or a failure to achieve "purpose." Other naturalisms work through an implicit anthropomorphism, where deviation involves going against the norms of "man." This is the feature of most forms of *modern naturalism*, with the addition of avowing no supposed purpose and raising the question of laws, as in the case of modern physical laws of science, that refer to how things simply "are." How deviations function in such regard is paradoxical since they should not be "possible" as deviations. They should simply be the same laws at work but exemplifying a different morphology. A mutant, for example, is still simply a function of the ongoing mechanisms of biological reproduction with possible "selections" being put to the test of the sustainability of such laws.[7] It is a failure to understand this dimension of Darwinism that led to notions that human beings evolved from chimpanzees or notions that different groups of human beings, although living in the same time, were less evolved. From the perspective of natural selection, their being around, their survival, is sufficient. The teleological tendency continues, however, in the many portraits of human evolution, where the contemporary human being is treated as the apotheosis of the process. A more accurate portrait would place a question mark, perhaps a series of question marks, after *homo sapien*, since no one knows what the future holds. The only conclusion to adaptation is extinction.

We have come, then, to the philosophical significance of monsters as emerging through the challenges they pose to notions of normativity and conceptions of the natural. What are monsters in such a world as ours, the contemporary modern age for many, postmodern one for others? What sense can we make of a warning when we avow no divine intelligence behind it?

We offer four immediate responses. The first is that there are supposedly natural signs and catastrophes whose meaning as warning is metaphorical. Think of the tremor over a fault line, the rising temperature of the planet, or the increased mercury in fish. The second is a reassertion of the old problem of theodicy. The term, as we have seen, refers to G-d's justice. Since G-d is supposed to be omnipotent, omniscient, and good, at least as understood in the African and West Asian civilizations from which the "world religions" of Judaism, Christianity, and Islam emerged, what must we conclude from the existence of injustice and evil?[8] The two classic responses basically exonerate G-d by asking: (1) who are we to question G-d's actions, given our finite knowledge? And (2), why should G-d be responsible after giving us free will? Why should G-d receive blame for human actions? Being free to commit good or evil means human responsibility for either. Both these responses refer to *human* limitations and capacities. The discussion of deviation thus returns in a formulation of injustice and evil as phenomena *beyond* G-d's actions. Although appealing to G-d (or the gods) is not legitimate according to modern naturalism, the *argument* still persists, where deviation becomes that which must be rationalized away as *external* to nature or any social system to which we adhere. The third is exemplified, as we have seen, in Simone Weil's remarkable essay, "The Love of God and Affliction."[9] Weil argues that mechanistic necessity and affliction force an emptying process of the soul, which she calls *de-creation*, beneath the lamentations of which "is the pearl of the silence of God."[10] This view does not push G-d to the nether regions of responsibility but to the heart of it and insists on the compatibility of G-d and physical reality. The fourth, related to the third, is one of the ways in which we endow natural phenomena with meaning in the ordinary sphere of human life—namely, through the resources, poetic and symbolic, of myth.

Myth, we should understand, has an impact on our lives beyond the prosaic notion of its referring to things that do not exist. It also involves that which brings meaning to the complex web of signs and symbols that constitute the meaningful world, that of norms and of what and how we insist the world must be by virtue of how we understand what it means for things to be at all. It has, in the language of Ernst Cassirer, its own *symbolic form*, or structure, which manifests itself as an organizing schema of reality. As Cassirer explains:

> It is one of the first essential insights of critical philosophy that objects are not "given" to consciousness in a rigid, finished state, in their naked "as suchness," but that the relation of representation to object presupposes an independent, spontaneous act of consciousness. The object does not exist prior to and outside of synthetic unity but is constituted only by this synthetic unity; it is no fixed form that imprints itself on consciousness but is the product of a formative operation effected by the basic instrumentality of consciousness, by intuition and pure thought. The *Philosophy of Symbolic Forms* takes up this basic critical idea, this fundamental principle of Kant's "Copernican revolution," and strives to broaden it. It seeks the categories of the consciousness of objects in the theoretical, intellectual sphere, and starts from the assumption that such categories must be at work wherever a cosmos, a characteristic and typical world view, takes form out of the chaos of impressions.[11]

Myth, in our context, brings meaning to this chaos of signs, the sign continuum, by making it symbolic. In *An Essay on Man*, Cassirer formulates the distinction and transformation illustratively as follows:

> For the sake of a clear statement of the problem we must carefully distinguish between *signs* and *symbols*. That we find rather

complex systems of signs and signals in animal behavior seems to be an ascertained fact. We may even say that some animals, especially domesticated animals, are extremely susceptible to signs. A dog will react to the slightest changes in the behavior of his master; he will even distinguish the expressions of a human face or the modulations of a human voice. But it is a far cry from these phenomena to an understanding of symbolic and human speech. The famous experiments of Pavlov prove only that animals can easily be trained to react not merely to direct stimuli but to all sorts of mediate or representative stimuli. A bell, for example, may become a "sign for dinner," and an animal may be trained not to touch its food when this sign is absent. But from this we learn only that the experimenter, in this case, has succeeded in changing the food-situation of the animal. He has complicated this situation by voluntarily introducing into it a new element. All the phenomena which are commonly described as conditioned reflexes are not merely very far from but even opposed to the essential character of human symbolic thought. Symbols—in the proper sense of this term—cannot be reduced to mere signals. Signals and symbols belong to two different universes of discourse: a signal is a part of the human world of meaning. Signals are "operators"; symbols are "designators." Signals, even when understood and used as such, have nevertheless a sort of physical or substantial being; symbols have only a functional value.[12]

Cassirer's work speaks to the structural order by which meaning, brought to belief, constitutes reality. As Claude Lévi-Strauss affirms, the symbolic structure "is specifically human, and ... is carried out according to the same laws among all men.... "[13] Lévi-Strauss is using *laws* in a specialized sense here. In these "laws," the physical and the mental collapse into a unity in which even biological forces echo belief, as his essay "The Sorcerer and His Magic" attests.[14] Myth here functions, however, in a multivariate structure or set of relations through which meaning is brought to human life. As such, it permeates even competing organizations of reality: "What makes a steel ax superior to a stone ax is not that the first one is better made than the second. They are equally well made, but steel is quite different from stone. In the same way we may be able to show that the same logical processes operate in myth as in science, and that man has always been thinking equally well; the improvement lies, not in an alleged progress of man's mind, but in the discovery of new areas to which it may apply its unchanged and unchanging powers."[15]

Our identification of the continued grammar of theodicy is one instance of the symbolic function or role of myth in which the secular and theological meet, and the organization of meaning in everyday life offers many examples. As Cavendish observes: "conflicting ideas about free-will, fate and luck, confidence in lucky charms, a feeling for omens and premonitions, and a hope that appeals to God may serve in desperate situations, are all jumbled together into a mixture found necessary in a society where both rationalism and religion are felt inadequate."[16] This underlying tension of fate and rationalism often continues through an ascription of the prevalence of one over the other in a conflict made manifest in competing myths. "Magic and divination are condemned in the Old Testament but, as usual," he adds, "it is private and authorized magic which is meant. Authorized magic was worked by prophets and priests who were instruments of God, like Moses and Aaron routing the Egyptian magicians in the contest before Pharaoh. Moses parted the Red Sea with his magic wand and struck water from a rock in the wilderness, but the marvels were God's doing. From an outside point of view, especially an Egyptian one, Moses was a powerful and distinctly sinister magician. From an Israelite point of view, he was a holy man and a servant of God."[17] We see here competing mythic organizations through which magic is pushed to the other side of each point of view in an economy to which we could add the additional terms of religion and science. "The religious impulse is to worship, the scientific to explain, the magical to dominate and command."[18] The ongoing reality of myth is not only the effort of religion and science to unveil the mythic underpinnings of each other but also the collusion of both at times against the threat of magic. Although magic is not our focus, the psychological impulse to which it speaks is linked to the mythic organization of response to the warnings of which we write. Peter Caws concurs, with slight differences: "Modern man thinks of these things [magic, myth, and totemism] as childish curiosities which he has long since outgrown, failing to see that science is his magic, literature and other forms of entertainment his myths, morality his totemism."[19]

The challenges raised by Lévi-Strauss and Cavendish, among others, can be extended to the scientific myth of producing knowledge without myth or of developing a myth-free methodology.[20] One needs to work through a form of coextensive analysis, where seemingly different things converge in the shared concept, since they operate within the life world of the human being, a word generative of many relations understood in relation to a continuous stream of other relations. What this means is that myths, although connected to avowed "laws" of human organization of symbolic life, resist generalizations that constitute a law of myths or mythic content as a closed or well-defined system—except, as we reflect on this consideration, as a negative claim of what myths do not do. As human phenomena, they are ongoing, evolving, transforming, open, and contingent realities. In other words, "The emergence of the human is the upsurge into the world of an intentional subjectivity, the contents of whose intentional domain are structured according to its own capacity for the positing and sustaining of relations."[21]

Defining monsters is much like defining myths. The phenomenon can become such an ongoing possibility of human existence, understood as an open series of relations, that even its rejection is one of its many instantiations. There is, then, no "law" of the monster outside of its production or conditions of its possibility. This is because monsters are, in many ways, ongoing achievements of deviation in the world created by human intersubjective activity, namely, the social world whose symbolic manifestation is culture, a world governed by meaning and ongoing efforts at order through structure.[22] Knowing that monsters are rooted in the notion of a warning explains the fear and anxiety they stimulate, as, for example, disruptions of systems and processes of relations, but it does not explain *what* would be the source of such a response and *how* it is read. As a consequence, a good way of going about the study of monsters is to leap into exemplars and thematize them into evolving types understood as dynamic generators of meaning.

The most ancient monsters will, of course, be those in Africa in the first 180,000 years of our species, should we subscribe to the view that human beings have been around for about 220,000 years. The complex experiences of those ancestors marked the organizing semiotics of the human world. Much of those experiences are left to our deeply rooted understanding of the most ancient, or perhaps primeval, human consciousness, and through the layers of sounds, signs, inscriptions; meteorological and geological events; zoological changes; and all that constitutes the natural history of the earth, they come to us in the mythopoetics and grammar of life itself as we know it today. What is clear is that the animal life of the planet was far richer then, so the scale and variety of living things from which to draw on for notions of things normal and deviant were greater. That phase, and the one up to about 30,000 or 20,000 years ago was thus zoomorphic. We know this from figurines of hippopotami and other creatures, in forms peculiar to human conceptions of fertility at the time, and also from the variety of creatures that operate in mythic life in the Nile Valley and artifacts along southern Asia and the Pacific regions that include the continent of Australia.[23]

The "monster" in stories from these earlier periods of human history is usually a function of enmity between the gods; it is usually a figure that disrupts harmony and brings chaos. The Egyptian god Set, who later became Satan and the Devil in Christian religions, and the dragon goddess Tiamat of the Babylonian myths, are examples; similar figures emerge in ancient (40,000 years old) Australian Aboriginal galleries in northern Australia in the form of the Rainbow Serpent.[24]

There is also the monstrous act, which makes sense, given the notion of monsters as deviation and the notion of a divine warning. Killing one's brother (Set among the Egyptians, Cain among the Hebrews), sleeping with one's mother (Oedipus with Jocasta among the ancient Greeks being the most discussed), and preventing the birth of subsequent generations (Ouranos among the same) are three examples, but what is odd about these actions in mythic life is that they have a form of necessity: The act is wrong but necessary, perhaps for the species, which makes the monster who commits this act a form of sacrifice or offering of self-sacrifice because of what is wrought upon him, her, or it. Such stories suggest a paradox about the consequences of ignoring such warning. The consequence of nearly all these tales is some notion of the present condition of humankind. The monster and monstrosity, in other words, appear linked to the scapegoat in whose banishment or destruction justice and order are restored. He, she, or it *must be sent out, punished, tortured, or even destroyed, for the sake of the community's effort to restore harmonious actions.*[25] In many instances, the community's sake is elusive and often metaphysical. Thus, the actual consequences beyond the actions unleashed on the monster, with the consequence of eclipsing the monster itself, are often irrelevant.

The determination of the monster on the basis of a monstrous act means that such monsters are linked to some notion of justice. Think of the ancient Greek concept of *dikaisounê*, that is, justice, setting things right, which has roots in the Egyptian notion of *Ma'at*, which not only means the same thing but is also, in similar kind, linked to balance and measurement, and the kind of beings who emerge as deviation from them. Even in recent times, the goddess Justice in western countries is not only blind but also brandishes a scale.[26] The theme of balance returns, but the concept of justice behind it offers no solace for the monster.

Extreme images from our primeval past and the emergence of monstrous actions led to a variety of ancient monsters whose grammar reaches the symbolic forms of the present. Recall that monsters are always extreme manifestations of things, and they are always out to get you (*i.e.*, "man"). This is a function of their excessiveness and status as a warning. Again, when they are around, something is wrong. With regard to extremes, the transition from occupying one's space to taking up too much room is, in effect, one of consuming one's surroundings. A quintessential example is the Cyclops in Homer's *Odyssey*. He is large, has one eye, and eats human beings. The feminine ones, such as the sirens and mermaids, are similar since they are powerful, hybrids of fish, and they lure men to a horrible death. By being able to occupy land and sea, they are without boundaries and thus consuming; in some versions, they eat their victims. The West African version has gone through many permutations, most of which are embodied by the goddess Mami Wata (mother water). She is often found at the shore (land and sea), and she offers wealth with fidelity as her price. Should one's infidelity arise, the price is death, at times through being dragged into the sea. Oddly enough, the Earth could be considered a mermaid since it embodies both land and sea and, by the end of the day, consumes all, not only as exemplified by death and decay but also by the price all of us pay for her ecological mistreatment.[27]

Then there are demonic creatures. Demons are monsters that deviate from spiritual naturalism, namely, the gods' or G-d's standards of right and wrong, and they spend much of their time luring men and women into such a fate. Deviation from G-d is, of course, bad to a scale of evil depending on how great the distance, and doing so also means to step out of one's proper place, which, in effect, carries the threat of "spreading," of extending one's reach. The science fiction horror film *The Blob* (1958; see also the 1988 remake) takes this insight to its material conclusions as the featured creature absorbs nearly every living thing in its path. Demonic monsters, at least in the Christian world, as we have seen, have many extensions to all things evil. Thus, witches, vampires, werewolves, anything created by curses are such monsters, although in some cultures the notion of a "witch" has a good and a bad form, but in such instances the term is more like that of genius, where there are good and evil geniuses.[28]

There are also monstrous ancestors—people from the past who are angry and in some way haunt the present. In African and Asian cultures and their Diaspora, they are creatures that are more than ghosts, since they are physical, present, and angry. The Europeans call them ghosts, but the metaphysics is dualistic since they materialize as crossing both a spiritual and a physical world. For these other communities, it is more along a spectrum from a potent and very real world to a less potent although real one, which affects the meaning of the entities that occupy the spectrum, especially those situated in the past and closer to metaphysical potency. Among the Akan of Ghana and many other central African communities, for instance, ancestors are closer to the time in which G-d gave all things being, and because of their proximity, they receive more of such reality-forming emanations.[29] No ancestor is worse, from such a view, than those whose anger was born close to the dawn of time.

Modern monsters are also dominated by a dual logic of (modern) naturalism and the syntax and mythopoetics of the past. *Monstrous creatures* become anything too large and dangerous, such as very big sharks, large crocodiles, and long snakes, or even giant people, as mythic representations of probably historical people such as Goliath in the Bible or fictional ones such as the giant in "Jack and the Beanstalk" attest. Morbidly fat people face, in addition to disgust, the wrath of those seeking salvation, as R. Marie Griffith observed:

"Fat People Don't Go To Heaven!" screamed a boldface headline inside the *Globe*, a national weekly tabloid circulated to millions of American readers. The story beneath this lurid caption in November 2000 recounted the rise of Gwen Shamblin, the founder and CEO of the nation's largest Christian diet company and recent subject of extensive press coverage from *Larry King Live* and *20/20* to the *New Yorker*. While this media flurry fed on controversies then swirling around Shamblin—including a series of lawsuits filed by former employees whom Shamblin allegedly fired for refusing to join her newly founded church—reporters reacted more to her stringent guidelines for proper Christian body size and their widespread popular reception. "I am not a savvy businessperson," Shamblin had lately pronounced in a front-page *Wall Street Journal* feature. "I'm just a dumb blonde with a genuine heart for God, who found the golden product that everyone wanted." That coveted discovery, a spiritual route to guaranteed weight loss, was marketed in the Weight Down Workshop, whose Shamblin-packed videos, audiotapes, books, conferences, and twelve-week seminars taught restrained eating as a divine command. The eternal costs of overeating were markedly severe: "Grace," in Shamblin's words, "does not go down into the pigpen."[30]

A recent monster from the animal kingdom was an extraordinarily large crocodile named Gustave that terrorized nearly every living thing along Lake Tanganyika in Burundi, Africa, for about thirty years into the end of the twentieth century.[31] One herpetologist who saw the creature for the first time on videotape gasped while she described it as "prehistoric." In such an assessment, we see the theme of transgressing place, of crossing time; the creature did not belong in the present. The movie *Jaws* (1975) offers a fictional account with much insight into our fears of large sharks. Yet ironically, things too small can also be dangerous and paradoxically monstrous, since they are presumed to harbor resentment against humanity for their size. Here, desire takes the place of action, although the presumption is that such kinds of behavior await their fruition. Thus, dwarfs, midgets, and short men (Napoleon Bonaparte, the eponym of a complex), "pygmies," and the like, although often made fun of, are also feared as monstrous creatures that, because of their small size, are angry at all things "normal," and that anger offers an avalanche of monstrous thoughts. Microorganisms such as death-causing bacteria and viruses are tiny, uncaring monsters. Perhaps the best recent example of a micro-monster is the HIV virus, which has been read by some communities as a divine warning or admonition of social behavior that transgresses their religious norms.

Most, if not all, deviants are at some point interpreted as monsters or warnings, although it would be a mistake to confuse deviancy with monstrosity. In our reading, the added dimension of warning, of appealing to deeper forces gone wrong, takes deviance to the realm of the monstrous, which, unfortunately for deviants, usually arises at moments of their efforts to assert human membership or, worse, at assimilation. The failure of assimilated deviance is what their presence signifies in the ongoing function of normality; they could only cease to be a dysfunctional sign through the transformative effect they have on functional, or at least believed to be functional, systems. In her thoughtful study of the mythic life of gender, Vered Lev Kenaan affirms our observation when, writing on the ancient Greek myth of Pandora, the first woman, she reflects: "In the beginning there were only men. Then came the first woman and disrupted the self-sameness that grounded the harmonious condition of humanity. Pandora appears in the world and immediately takes the form of the ultimate Other. But the fact that she bears the mark of otherness is due not only to her femininity or to her sexuality as such. Pandora is a gift. Her appearance in the world is the appearance of something given to men. She is not an inherent element of the world, not a daughter of nature. The first woman lacks the autochthonic roots of men. Pandora presents a new mode of being in the world that stands in opposition to the natural being of men."[32] The myth of woman as deviance is not limited to Greek antiquity. Genesis II has offered the prevailing model in Jewish, Christian, and Muslim interpretations of woman, where Lev Kenaan's observation finds exemplars in Lilith and Eve, wives of Adam, the second of whom is more known. Eve emerges after Adam, fashioned by G-d from one of his ribs during a state of sleep, symbolic of unconsciousness and death, which, as Schopenhauer argued, is an absence of evil: "for every evil, like every good, presupposes existence, indeed even consciousness. But this ceases with life, as well as in sleep and in a fainting fit; therefore the absence of consciousness is well known and familiar to us as a state containing no evil at all.... Epicurus considered death from this point of view, and therefore said quite rightly: ['Death does not concern us'], with the explanation that when we are, death is not, and when death is, we are not."[33]

The Hebrew view attributes all creation to G-d, which offers an interpretation of assured absence of agency from Adam, even though Eve is formed from him. The "blame," so to speak, belongs to G-d, which raises a theodicean problem the extent to which woman is understood as evil. Along the social understanding of Adam as the given condition of normality, the absence of his agency places the emergence of Eve in the realm of affliction. But, as we have seen, affliction, too, has a theodicean dimension. Expanding the theme of deviation, however, is the difference between Genesis II, where Eve is introduced, and Genesis I, where G-d made woman and man at the same time, without, in other words, an ontological or cosmogenic hierarchy. Genesis is made consistent, however, in the myth of Lilith, the missing, developed story, wherein the woman in Genesis I is perhaps not Eve.[34] Eve was, in this interpretation, created after Lilith was banished from

Eden because of her insolence and failure to be subservient. She became a demon, in some versions a vampire who preys upon babies in the night. The choice of fashioning Eve from one of Adam's rib, a bone without which he could survive, was supposedly to ensure her subservience. That failure affirms our point of systemic dysfunction. The failure is, however, paradoxical, for without the additional disobedience wrought from the realization of freedom to defy G-d through eating from the fruit of knowledge, what would humanity be? Lilith and Eve, in their suffering, also gave birth, as symbols, of the ongoing, unfolding of symbols, incomplete, contingent, fallen, but also recognizable as the "we" to whom responsibility for meaning makes, in a word, sense.[35]

Gender deviance, born in the genesis of antiquity, reached across the ages to racial deviance, which was in turn born in the formation of the modern world. Such deviance is *of* this epoch in ways that appeal to its foundations. As *Birth of a Nation* (1915) illustrated—black people, the quintessential racial deviants of the modern world, so because they often eclipse other racial groups in the iconography of race, are monsters in antiblack societies, or at least so when they attempt to live and participate in the wider civil society and engage in processes of governing among whites; all is excess to the point of transgressing laws and mores in a rapacious overflow of lust and greed. That cinematic portrayal of black senators during the period of Reconstruction after the U.S. Civil War included images of those congressmen, barefoot and unkempt, eating fried chicken and watermelons while in session and of a lusty black rapist chasing a white woman to her death. The grammar of such monstrosity no doubt animates the semiotics and practice of incarceration; blacks, being by definition illicit, exemplify legitimate imprisonment. Their presence *in* society generally constitutes crime.[36]

There are, as well, monsters of sexual deviance, as homosexuals are in a world that renders heterosexuality as both natural and normative and other forms of sexuality deviant; in Euripides' satyr play *The Cyclops* (420 BCE), the one-eyed creature Polyphemus not only eats men but also sodomizes them, as this passage of his lust for the old man/satyr Silenus demonstrates:

CYCLOPS
The Graces tempt me! My Ganymede here
(*He grabs Silenus.*)
is good enough for me. With him I'll sleep
magnificently. By these Graces, I will!

And anyway, I prefer boys to girls.
SILENUS
Am I Zeus' little Ganymede, Cyclops?
CYCLOPS
You are, by Zeus! The boy I stole from Dardanos!
SILENUS
I am done for, children. Foul things await me.
CYCLOPS
Sneer at your lover, do you, because he's drunk?
SILENUS
It's a bitter wine I'll have to drink now.
(*Cyclops drags off Silenus protesting into the cave.*)[37]

For ancient Greek audiences, it was not the question of bestiality that would have been at issue but the upset hierarchy of an older man being penetrated not only by a lesser creature but also a younger one (signifying further humiliation). All these themes come together in the vampire. Although vampires in principle belong to no race or ethnic group more than others, their adaptation into English society and then American popular film culture first took the form of xenophobic and anti-Semitic iconography from the Middle Ages and subsequent fears of migration occasioned by an expanded Europe.[38] *Nosferatu* (1922) and *Dracula* (novel, 1897; Hollywood version, 1931), for example, reveal Semitic monsters for the European and American anti-Semite. Those vampires are, after all, soulless Jews who bring plagues, pursue the gentile female, prey upon the young (given the near ancient age of the creature), and fear the cross (Christianity). Béla Lugosi's costume for the 1931 cinematic version, for instance, included a medallion Magen David or Star of David.[39] The mythic foundations of *Dracula* clearly reach, however, beyond the emergence of anti-Semitism, in that we see here the familiar dynamic of the bad, incestuous father who will not permit access to the daughters by younger men (the sons). In making his brides into vampires, Dracula is both their father and their lover, and we see in this story, through the heroic role of Jonathan Harker and the other young men who hunt down the vampire, the familiar tale—which haunts even superhero films—of the youthful hero acquiring the beautiful maiden by destroying the older villain (the father) who lusted after her. There is, however, a twist to this story if we push its themes further. Dracula, read as also a pimp, makes his daughters/lovers into whores, and he achieves this through oral sex, the perhaps most requested sexual act for prostitutes worldwide.[40] The twist, of course, is that Dracula both gives and receives oral sex, and so do his brides/daughters, who seek to drink not only from men but also from women. It is a world of unbound sexuality (radical queerness) premised upon the pleasures of the mouth and the seduction of being consumed. In less grandiose form, *syphilitic* women and those who are governed by their pleasures obey few (if any) boundaries and are thus also monsters, sometimes presented as vampires but nearly always as "man-eaters." The film *Basic Instinct* (1992) illustrates this point well. And, at the level of our own bodies, there is the monster of "fat" or obesity. Such a monstrosity is a warning to each of us of the perils of extreme consumption, as we saw in the Evangelic threat of fat people being barred from heaven.

A more complex monster in the modern age is the genius. Extreme intelligence suggests a monstrosity exemplified best by the mad scientist but is expressed in many forms. The artistic genius is, after all, also one who deviates from norms, although he or she knows very well such "laws." Immanuel Kant, arguably one of, if not *the* greatest genius of modern German philosophy, defines genius thus: "*Genius* is the talent (natural endowment) that gives the rule to art. Since talent is an innate productive ability of the artist and as such belongs itself to nature, we could also put it this way: *Genius* is the innate mental disposition (*ingenium*) *through which* nature gives the rule of art."[41] Later, he reflects on this subject with near contempt for what, given his stature and expectations of his thought as science more than art, was autobiographical based on his arguments for the active role of mind, or at least its structure, in the formation of concepts:

> Accordingly, the product of a genius (as regards what is attributable to genius in it rather than to possible learning or academic instruction) is an example that is meant not to be imitated, but to be followed by another genius. ... This courage [to retain deformities] has merit only in a genius. A certain *boldness* of expression, and in general some deviation from the common rule, is entirely fitting for a genius; it is however not at all worthy of imitation, but in itself always remains a defect that [any] one must try to eliminate, though the genius has, as it were, a privilege to allow the defect to remain [anyway], because the inimitable [element] in the momentum of his spirit would be impaired by timorous caution.[42]

Kant was here speaking of artistic genius, which he contrasted with scientific talent, which "lies in continuing to increase the perfection of our cognitions and of all the benefits that depend on [these], as well as in imparting that same knowledge to others; and in these respects they are far superior to those who merit the honor of being called geniuses."[43] Kant's anxieties over the artistic genius no doubt took similar form in those for whom his talent, scientific and philosophical, must have equally been a mystery. It no doubt stimulated, as some of his colleagues reflected upon themselves, fear and trembling. No wonder the stories of Kant's obsessive attachment to order and regularity became staples of his biography.[44] This focus on Kant's obsessive behavior is not far afield from some recent efforts to explain genius. In *Genius Explained*, Michael A. J. Howe reminds us, for instance, in a sociologically Protestant reading of the phenomenon, that although the world has seen many prodigies, not all of them turned out to be geniuses, and there have been and continue to be geniuses who were not prodigies.[45] The determination of their genius was, he argues, from what they produced; what many geniuses also have in common are environmental conditions conducive to their work, special personalities, and a penchant for hard work. Focusing on savants, Oliver Sacks, drawing upon the research of the psychologist Howard Gardner and recent research in neurology, reads geniuses and savants as manifesting, in a more unusual and intense way, faculties shared by most of us and often lacking, in similarly unusual and intense ways, dimensions necessary for well-integrated social life and human development. "The other side of the prodigiousness and precocity, the unchildlikeness, of savant gifts," he writes, "is that they do not seem to develop as normal talents do. They are fully fledged from the start.... It may be that savants have a highly specialized, immensely developed system in the brain, a 'neuromodule' and that this is 'switched on' at particular times—when the right stimulus (musical, visual, whatever) meets the system at the right time—and immediately starts to operate full blast."[46]

In the twentieth century, Einstein became an eponym for genius. Although he was quite a handsome and sociable man, Albert Einstein is more remembered by photographs of him as a disheveled and tired geriatric after years of struggling to formulate a proper response to quantum mechanics. That image of pushed-back, unkempt gray hair and the wrinkled forehead became the quintessential portrait of the mad scientist, although a white lab coat takes the place of his wool sweater in the portrayal of many such scientists. It is as if to say of Einstein that there was something *wrong* with him, that the power of his brain made the rest of him, and his life, off balance. Roland Barthes concurs, when he writes:

> Einstein's brain is a mythical object: paradoxically, the greatest intelligence of all provides an image of the most up-to-date machine, the man who is too powerful is removed from psychology, and introduced into a world of robots.... [Since] God's share must be preserved, some failure on the part of Einstein is necessary: Einstein died, it is said, without having been able to verify *'the equation in which the secret of the world was enclosed'.* So in the end the world resisted; hardly opened, the secret closed again, the code was incomplete. In this way Einstein fulfils all the conditions of myth, which could not care less about contradictions so long as it establishes a euphoric security: at once magician and machine, eternal researcher and unfulfilled discoverer, unleashing the best and the worst, brain and conscience, Einstein embodies the most contradictory dreams, and mythically reconciles the infinite power of man over nature with the 'fatality' of the sacrosanct, which man cannot yet do without.[47]

That conception of the genius, or at least what it means to be intellectually gifted, as a flawed being haunts the present in the form of nerdy, geeky images of such people, as if to say that their bodies are warnings of the dangers of overusing the mind. Such images are dominant although many of the greatest geniuses in history were athletic and, at times, physically beautiful. Even Plato, whose actual name was Aristokles, reputedly earned his better-known nickname because of his broad shoulders, which he developed from his favorite sport: wrestling.

A particularly feared modern monster combines racial deviation and genius. It is the person who exemplifies an achievement of modernity but is of the kind thought not to be capable of it. Such individuals are accused of having done something wrong *because it must be so.* They are, in effect, modern-day witches, demonic creatures, or practitioners of unauthorized magic. An example of this is the logic of "disqualification" used in anti-affirmative action rhetoric. What excludes races requires racial criteria, but since appealing to such is considered illegitimate in liberal societies, its use to identify the recipient with whom to respond to the injustice loses its legitimacy as well. In effect, the supposed absence of qualification is really more about the recipient than actual credentials. We know this since the mediocrity of those who exclude the minority recipient is not called into question, just as the many invisible extraordinary individuals (from the minority group) who are either passed over in selections processes or, if selected, no longer count as authentic instances of the excluded. The result, for the recipient of affirmative action, is the rejection of the ordinary; he or she must be extraordinary not to receive the wrath of anti-affirmative action critics, even though they do not make such complaints when ordinary members of the dominant group are selected for the relevant posts.[48] The "Catch 22" follows: To qualify, a member of a racial minority must be extraordinary, but if he or she is extraordinary, then that person is not the norm. Thus, deviation becomes the only legitimate recourse. Recent research, such as those of the anthropologists Jean Comaroff and John Comaroff, show a rise in the number of people accused of being "witches" in places with high expectations from capitalism in an emancipating moment with the people subsequently suffering low yields.[49] Much of the logic around "harassment" in the work place in recent times takes this form as well, where many men of color are accused because of the mere fact that their presence, echoing *Birth of a Nation,* makes their (mostly white but not exclusively so) female colleagues uncomfortable because they are, by definition, endangered; most "harassers," and even those innocently accused of it, are, in the end, also considered to be monsters and are often referred to as "predators," where the range from physical assault to the verbal pass or simply aggressively saying nothing is blurred.[50] These circumstances lead inevitably to the notion of political monsters, which, in some sense, all monsters ultimately are. In the War on Terror, the term "radical" is used to refer to terrorists in ways that do not distinguish the radical left from the radical right. That the actual attacks have been by the radical right is elided by a policy that devotes more energy to eliminating the radical left. This is consistent with the mythic underbelly of a world where such a word as "sinister," which, in Latin, means "left" or "to the left," versus such words as "rectify" (to make right, from *rectus,* which means "straight"), "rectitude" (uprightness, also from *rectus*), and "recto" (on the right). These words all relate to *regere* (to guide, to rule), which reveals why, on matters of things radical, although the right may be to the extreme, it is the left who receives the charge of monstrosity. This is because, as well, the mere existence of the left is a warning; whereas the right wants to set things straight, to return; the left is an announcement of an end, a collapse of forces whose demise means to face the future in a way that portends the death of the present and the past, in the emergence of the new and, hence, the unknown. This reasoning is the *philosophical source* of political right and left distinctions. As noted in the previous chapter, the initial designations were arbitrary, a function of seating arrangements in the French Parliament distinguishing the monarchists and republicans in the eighteenth century. What is significant here is the mythic organization of symbols mapped onto that distinction. The grammar of Western civilization is such that the left would receive the ancient organization of symbols outlined here.

Finally, although not exhaustively, there are *nihilistic monsters.* These are the monsters whose logic is an eternal return of indifference and an absence of meaning. The Nietzschean motif here is not accidental. Nihilism, Nietzsche argued, is symptomatic of the values of a decaying society.[51] It is not that monsters in such a society are bad or good; they simply "are," which in the course of things means that the boundaries lack meaning for them beyond their natural purpose, which often, as in the other instances, means to consume. They are not after you, since they do not, in the end, care about you, for they do not know who "you" are in your uniqueness, and even if they did, they would not care, simply because, as well, that does not concern them.[52] Such monsters reflect another nihilistic value, at least as Nietzsche regarded a decadent society: egalitarianism. Such monsters discriminate against no one. Even the monsters themselves are, in the end, equal. Contemporary zombies, the walking dead driven by hunger are such monsters. They are death, the logical conclusion of decay, brought to unnatural heights in the added dimension of being *the living dead.*

Recent developments of zombie imagery have been distinguished by, among other things, a transition from *the zombie* to *zombies.* In the past, the creature, born from voodoun and other Afro-Caribbean religions, was simply a human being who was made a slave by the theft of his or her soul or, in other versions, an animated corpse at the mercy of the will of those who summoned it. The latter version spawned such films as *White Zombie* (1932) and *I Walked with a Zombie* (1943). We are, however, living in times when the living are beginning to outnumber the dead, which threatens the meaning behind Ishtar's ancient Sumerian admonition in *The Epic of Gilgamesh:*

> Father give me the Bull of Heaven,
> So he can kill Gilgamesh in his dwelling.
> If you do not give me the Bull of Heaven,

I will knock down the Gates of the Netherworld,
I will smash the doorposts, and leave the doors flat down,
and will let the dead go up to eat the living!
And the dead will outnumber the living![53]

Zombies now come in *crowds*, and their consuming aim is no less than human population control. The plenitude of such monsters exemplifies that overflowing indifference or nature's "will," as Arthur Schopenhauer might put it, which is uncaring and unceasing.[54] The classic exemplar of this development is the original *Night of the Living Dead* (1968), where a zombie consumes his living sister; a zombie daughter kills (one cannot say "murders" since she herself is dead) and consumes her parents; and the black protagonist, after surviving a night of fighting zombies as well as selfish and desperate members of the living, is shot to death while walking sluggishly (zombie-like) through the house. The men who shot him could not be blamed since he was moving like a zombie, and to add to the nihilistic elements, his body is thrown on a heap of burning zombies who have been immobilized by a shot in the head. There is, as well, the added rub: In spite of his heroism, which reveals that he is a greater man than most, his killers were, in the end, very ordinary men.

Sociopaths and psychopaths are similar to zombies. Nothing that follows is a function of care or concern; the logic of the eternal returning psychopathic killer is a theme in cinema as well as the mythopoetics of contemporary life. The blind, masked killers of *Texas Chainsaw Massacre* (1974; remake 2003), *Halloween* (1978; sequels still counting), and *Friday the 13th* (1980; and sequels also still counting), in addition to real-life serial killers, all return in sequels even for their sequels. Those monsters are "out there," driven, in the end, more by their nature than are the rest of us who are moved by ethics and social mores, with their message of nihilism, reminding us of decaying values, of our creating a world in which, in the end, not only nothing, but *no one* really matters.

Our analysis suggests that we should examine how monsters operate in mundane life and their significance as objects of consciousness or their meaning as phenomena of the social world. An obvious, early result pertains to untamed nature and nihilistic monsters in the modern world. A distinct feature of First World society, for instance, is the phenomenon of constant human interaction with animals. From the perspective of many people from poorer countries, it seems that First World people love their animals more than they do (if at all) other human beings, and there are those who confess to holding such a position.[55] Even more striking is how people in North America and Europe seem no longer to be afraid of animals. They have, in effect, eliminated their "wild," which means, as well, the rejection of the notion of wild animals. (There are North American and European tourists who are mauled or killed by such animals as crocodiles in Australia or attacked by bears and cougars in North America as those tourists choose either to swim in infested lakes or walk along wilderness trails by themselves or, even worse, seek out the animals for such contact.) It is no accident that in such countries, the notion of the "wild" is associated more with kinds of human beings, often blacks and indigenous peoples, whom they treat, paradoxically, as animals while denying animality to actual, non-human creatures.

The emergence of nihilistic monsters suggests a death of values, which includes values of knowledge. Yet paradoxically, as a *warning*, monsters always mean that there is something that the human community can do, that things have not gone *too far*. Even in nihilistic zombie films, *someone* survives, even if it is not the one the audience might have been rooting for. But the fate of that survivor is one of a constant fear of reaching out to others. What this dimension of the nihilistic threat means is that *no one* can be trusted, and in such a situation, the monstrous rises as the normative condition of paranoid reality: The ultimate monsters become those whom we once, before such a development, dared to love.

◊

3

Creatures

We have thus far outlined a typology of monsters comprised of three basic types. Ancient monsters, those that ground the mythopoetics of more contemporary ones, are figures that, as a function of enmity between the gods, disrupt harmony, bringing chaos. These frequently take their form in a monstrous act—killing a brother or sleeping with one's mother—that is wrong but the correction of which is necessary for the life of the community. The destruction of the monster therefore becomes a form of sacrifice. He or she must be destroyed for the sake of the community. All such monsters deviate from G-d's or the gods' standards of right and wrong, beckoning to others to do the same.

Modern monsters combine a dual logic of modern naturalism with the syntax of the past in the form of monstrous creatures. These are strangely things that are naturally unnatural, such as people or animals or any other sort of creature that is too large or too small, or even too smart. Although deviancy and monstrosity are not identical, all deviants of the modern world are, at some point, interpreted, as we have seen, as warnings of deeper forces gone wrong. Consider how it is that nineteenth-century European Jews were blamed simultaneously for being too ancient and too modern a people, as being fanatically local and parochial and of sustaining parasitic international networks that their contemporaries could not fathom, of being the essential Bolsheviks and the ultimate capitalists. Of particular interest here are those creatures that either combine more than one form of deviation, such as being black and a genius, or attributes that are not supposed to merge, as in the case of a female genius. Although it is not our focus in what follows, this discussion is also clearly linked to another, of individuals that belong to multiple groups that have been defined as discrete kinds of deviants. For instance, anxieties frequently emerge even over racial-ethnic and religious deviance converging in an individual or community as is the case of black or Afro-Jews, people who, in one body, are perceived to be at once excessively corporeal and extremely cerebral. This identity, for many, is what Frantz Fanon suggested the antiblack racist perceived in the figure of an educated black man, namely, at the level of imagination, Rodin's *The Thinker* with a permanent erection.[1] It is no wonder that the response of so many non-black Jews and non-Jews to black Jews is to suggest that either their blackness or their Jewishness cannot be real, that it must be feigned or inauthentically adopted, that they cannot be "natural" features of the modern world.[2]

Then there are nihilistic monsters that embody an absolute indifference to or absence of meaning. There is no normative content in their behavior, because the meaning of both good and bad in the contexts in which they appear lack coherence. If anything, they are excessively egalitarian, but here in the sense criticized earlier by José Ortega y Gasset: they are antagonistic to any of the rules or standards that are necessary to give a formless mass the shape of a community or an idea. The zombie, for instance, is hungry or destructive. There is nothing unique or particular about its victims. They are nothing other than mere flesh to be mangled or devoured. This exemplifies a form of nihilism in whose wake is a death of values, including the values of knowledge, indicative of the postmodern age. Rather than monstrous agents, perceived to endanger shared values, reminding those that embody them that their content could be otherwise, postmodern monsters force those around them to imagine predicaments in which meaningful social worlds were destroyed by creatures that function as mere mechanism, the law-like and consistent playing out of naturalistic laws. These situations make us imagine the ultimate triumph of the disciplinary dreams of reductionistic empiricists, what Fanon depicted as "man's surrender," those that mock the very aspiration at the core of politics as we have described it, of forging meaningful social worlds that carve out values and temporalities that if not suspending, do not bow wholly to the dictates of biology and nature.[3]

We now explore these themes through an analysis of perhaps the most influential work of horror and science fiction and another in what is now known as postcolonial thought. One of the many unique features of Mary Shelley's *Frankenstein* and Frantz Fanon's *Black Skin, White Masks* is that in addition to exploring

the very literal creation of two instances of modern monsters—
in the case of Frankenstein's creature, a massive, lumbering
collage of corpses imbued with the breath of life, senses, and
intelligence; in the second, a black human being, debased in the
modern world as being devoid of humanity to the point of supposedly lacking an inner life—they also offer tragic autobiographical
accounts from the point of view and in the voice of the monsters
themselves. Although *Black Skin* ends much more optimistically,
with the hope of an alternative to being caught in the dialectics of
recognition with one's creator who shuns one by rendering white
normativity irrelevant, by way of an embodied interrogative, in the
reconstruction of the nature and meaning of modern mankind,
both narratives are punctuated by central tropes of failure. For
Shelley and Fanon, the violence that is understood to define the
monstrosity of the creatures on whom they focus is depicted as
being turned to as a last rather than first resort, as a response
to the inability of every other effort constructively to become part
of intersubjective life. The impossibility of doing this in any other
way but those perceived by the creatures and their creators as
negative does not itself provide any comfort to the perpetrators.
For Fanon, although indispensable to the forging of a legitimate
postcolonial nation, the blood on the hands of the national liberators leaves them damaged and unsuitable to lead in a future for
which they have made such a sacrifice. Frankenstein's creature,
although immortalized by the ways in which the novel has cap-
tured the imaginations of centuries of readers, tries to eliminate
any mark of his ever having existed, incinerating himself amidst
the insufferable cold of the Arctic North. Whereas Fanon asked
his body to make of him a man who questions, Frankenstein's
creature feared the knowledge locked in his body and thus, instead of praying for a question, sought erasure and the goal of
forgetting. He assured Walton, the explorer through whose letters the story unfolds, that his own hatred for himself surpasses
that of all others. He is incapable of what Fanon suggests opens
for the colonized in the trajectory of liberation; he cannot, as the
Algerian national liberators, vomit up the horribly ill-conceived
understandings of glory that brought him into being only to be
refused a fully human existence. Serving as a refrain for both the
creature and the colonized is the question the inassimilable person
is forced to ask in the face of repeated failures to become part of
the normative social world. In Fanon's thought this appears as,
"What, in reality, am I"? Frankenstein's creature, when seeing his

reflection and realizing that it really is his own, asked of himself, "And what was I?" It was a question, the creature recalled, that he could only answer with groans.[4] Both here echo W.E.B. Du Bois's classic reflections on how it feels to be a problem.

Walton's letters to his sister, Mrs. Seville, who shares the initials of the book's author, recount the entire story of *Frankenstein*, as the "divine wanderer"; the protagonist, Victor, a precocious Genevan raised by conscientiously republican parents, moved by his hunger to uncover the hidden laws of nature and the largely discredited pre-modern scientific writings of Cornelius Agrippa, Paracelsus, and Albertus Magnus, was taken at University by the idea, challenge, and potential glory of reanimating life, of banishing "death from the human frame and render[ing] man invulnerable to any but a violent death."[5] The otherwise outgoing and sociable man whose potential to become sullen or rough through ardor had been curbed by the influences of others, especially his adopted sister and his bride-to-be, Elizabeth Lavenza, became wrapped up obsessively in his endeavor, leaving his laboratory only to search through graveyards, vaults, and charnel-houses first to study decaying life and then for parts to piece together into the enormous creature that he indeed brings to life. Victor emphasized that he brought to the questions about the principles of life a supernatural enthusiasm that alone made possible the examination of death required to understand life. In addition to anatomy, this goal required investigating the corruption of the human body. He reflected, "In my education my father had taken the greatest precautions that my mind should be impressed with no supernatural horrors. I do not ever remember to have trembled at a tale of superstition, or to have feared the apparition of a spirit. Darkness had no effect upon my fancy; and a churchyard was to me merely the receptacle of bodies deprived of life, which, from being the seat of beauty and strength, had become food for the worm."[6] Having discerned the capacity of bestowing animation, feelings bore him on "like a hurricane." He would break through the bounds of life and death: "A new species would bless me as its creator and source; many happy and excellent natures would owe their being to me. No father could claim the gratitude of his child so completely as I should deserve theirs."[7] Driven on secretly and frantically, with loathing and eagerness, alone in his solitary workshop, he became numb to the charms of nature and memories of family and friends. He reflected later,

A human being in perfection ought always to preserve a calm and peaceful mind, and never to allow passion or a transitory desire to disturb his tranquility. I do not think that the pursuit of knowledge is an exception to this rule. If the study to which you apply yourself has a tendency to weaken your affections, and to destroy your taste for those simple pleasures in which no alloy can possibly mix, then that study is certainly unlawful, that is to say, not befitting the human mind. If this rule were always observed; if no man allowed any pursuit whatsoever to interfere with the tranquility of his domestic affections, Greece would not have been enslaved; Caesar would have spared his country; America would have been discovered more gradually; and the empires of Mexico and Peru had not been destroyed.[8]

This commentary was offered by Victor as counsel to Walton, who, at the time of their meeting was pursuing a course into the Arctic that no European man had yet been able to reach. The opening lines of the novel demonstrate that in so doing he has ignored the admonitions of his sister. Walton ultimately heeds Victor's warnings, concluding the story by doing what his sister, from the first, advised, but with much regret and the suggestion that he will try again. Victor, for his own part, had gone too far to reverse his course.

At the moment of the completion of nearly two years work, beholding "the accomplishment of [his] toils ... with an anxiety that almost amounted to agony," rather than feeling delight and triumph, he shuddered with fear and horror when the creature opened its yellow eye, revealing its own point of view, and looked at him. In "this catastrophe," he perceived the wretchedness of the body that he had so carefully formed. Victor rushed to his bedchamber hoping simply to forget. His psychoanalytically rich dreams of kissing a vibrant Elizabeth whose lips first turned to the color of death and then into the corpse of Victor's mother surrounded by a shroud crawling with grave-worms were interrupted by the creature, who, peering through the curtains of the bed, "muttered some inarticulate sounds, while a grin wrinkled his cheeks. He might have spoken, but I did not hear; one hand was stretched out, seemingly to detain me, but I escaped."[9] Victor rushed off, leaving behind his journal with its detailed account of his experimental endeavors. He wished that the creature would simply disappear. Sick from overwork and anguish, he was nursed first by his beloved friend, Henry Clerval, and then returned home after a long period of absence, desperately hoping that what he had done would fade as a bad dream.

The creature emerged through a blur of confused senses and sensations, alone, cold, desolate, and hungry. He left the lab only to discover that everyone he encountered recoiled at the sight of him with violent disgust and horror. He found his way to the woods and then to a hovel in which he took refuge beside a cottage in which the exiled De Lacey family lived. He developed deep affection for the members of the family and their lives, observing them for months, learning to speak through their studious observation, helping to collect wood for them, becoming, in his view, an invisible member of their family who tried, in every way that he could conceive, to minimize the misery of their poverty and dislocation. He hoped that his growing ability to speak would mitigate the visceral response that his appearance evoked.

"By degrees," he recalled,

> I made a discovery of still greater moment. I found that these people possessed a method of communicating their experience and feelings to one another by articulate sounds. I perceived that the words they spoke sometimes produced pleasure or pain, smiles or sadness, in the minds and countenances of the hearers. This was indeed a godlike science, and I ardently desired to become acquainted with it.[10]

But it proved very difficult: they pronounced words quickly and there seemed little or no apparent connection between the sounds and the objects to which they referred. Still, after many months of application, the creature discovered the most familiar of names. With great delight, he slowly learned the requisite sounds, devoting "his whole mind to the endeavor."[11] He worked as he did for he hoped to introduce himself to the cottagers but had concluded "not to make the attempt until I had first become master of their language; which knowledge might enable me to make them overlook the deformity of my figure."[12] Having seen himself in a clear pool, he had with despondence and mortification, as we have mentioned, realized that the monstrous reflection was his own. He imagined that with his "conciliating words" he could win their favor over and against this. He concluded that these "superior beings" would "be the arbiters of [his] future destiny."[13]

He prepared himself for an interview with them that would "decide [his] fate."[14] The more he learned, the more profound was his sense of himself as a wretched outcast and the greater became his hope that speaking could transform his condition. He learned through overhearing and through his own reading of the history of empire, weeping over the "hapless fate of the original inhabitants" of the American hemisphere, of the magnificent heights and base depths of which human beings were capable, that it was "high and unsullied descent united with riches" that were most esteemed but that without these most people were condemned to be vagabonds and slaves, "doomed to waste [their] powers for the profits of the chosen few."[15] He reflected that he knew nothing of his creation and creator and that he had neither friends nor money and that, in addition, he was deformed. "Was I then," he asked, "a monster, a blot upon the earth, from which all men fled and whom all men disowned?"[16] Much like Frederick Douglass, reflecting upon the ways in which his own developing literacy made him more aware of the profound injustices that gave U.S. slavery its form and content, the creature noted that his sorrow and agony increased with his knowledge. He wished, as did Douglass, that he could not have felt or known beyond the barest of biological necessities for food, drink, and warmth.[17]

Still, having seen that the cottagers never refused the poor visitors who stopped at their door asking for food and refuge, he hoped for himself. He identified with the isolation and misery of such visitors and hoped that the De Lacey family, who seemed not to blame the condition of marginality on marginal people themselves, would extend the same generosity to him. Still, he feared that his monstrosity was unique, not comparable with the poverty of social or political dislocation, but resisted resigning himself to such a conclusion. Having observed that "the unnatural hideousness of [his] person was the chief object of horror with those who had beheld it," he decided to enter the cottage when the blind old man, the family's patriarch, was alone.[18] He hoped that his voice, with "nothing terrible in it," would encourage the sympathy of the old De Lacey, who, on his behalf, could speak to his younger family. "[T]o see their sweet looks directed toward me with affection," he reflected, "was the utmost limit of my ambition."[19]

As with all idealized hopes, reality fell short. When the day finally arrived and with diffidence the creature knocked at and entered the cottage, describing his isolation to the old man whom he beseeched to help him to "undeceive" those for whom he had developed such affection, the younger family members suddenly returned. Upon seeing the creature, one fainted, while the other tore the creature away from his father, striking him with a stick.

Devastated, the creature disappeared into the woods and collapsed into sleep, hoping to return and in spite of what had just transpired, try yet again. When he awoke and returned, the cottage was empty and dark; hiding in the bushes, he heard the son explaining to his landlord that no losses could be too great, that the danger of remaining in their former home was to nothing less than their father's life. His wife and sister, the son explained, still had not recovered from their horror. The creature recalled, "My protectors had departed, and had broken the only link that held me to the world. For the first time the feelings of revenge and hatred filled my bosom."[20]

Knowing that his reception, wherever he might go, would be equally violent, the creature traveled at night in search of his creator, whom he knew by name through the work journal that he had left behind in his flight from the laboratory. The creature asked, "to whom could I apply with more fitness than to him who had given me life? ... From you only could I hope for succor, although towards you I felt no sentiment but that of hatred."[21]

Having endowed the creature with both perceptions and passions, Victor had then cast him aside. But it was with Frankenstein alone, the creature reflected, that he could make any claim for pity or redress, "from [him the creature] determined to seek that justice which [he] vainly attempted to gain from any other being that wore the human form."[22] Along his journey, temporarily moved by the loveliness of spring, he came out from hiding only to see and then rescue a little girl who, in play, had slipped into the water. When the girl's father appeared, without a word, he grabbed his daughter out of the creature's arms, retreated slightly, and fired his gun at the creature. Enraged by this injustice and ingratitude, the creature could not be soothed by the sun. "[A]ll joy," he commented, "was but a mockery which insulted my desolate state, and made me feel more painfully that I was not made for the enjoyment of pleasure."[23]

Having arrived in Geneva he is woken from "a slight sleep" by the approach of a small, beautiful boy running into the recess in which he hid. It occurred suddenly to the creature that the child might remain "unprejudiced," that he might not have yet lived long enough to have "imbibed a horror of deformity."[24] Perhaps he might educate the child as a companion and friend, ending his own absolute isolation. As the creature drew the boy toward him, however, the little boy's response was immediate and extreme. He screamed and struggled violently, crying "Monster! ugly wretch!

you wish to eat me and tear me to pieces—You are an ogre—Let me go, or I will tell my papa."[25] The boy threatened that his father, Doctor Frankenstein, would punish the creature and continued on with hateful epithets. Grasping the child's throat to silence him, the creature killed the boy in a moment. The creature, for the first time, embraced being *the monster,* doing what others expected of him, being what they claimed him to be. He declared, "I too can create desolation; my enemy is not invulnerable; this death will carry despair to him, and a thousand other miseries shall torment and destroy him."[26] Failing to forge positive relationships with other human beings and through them a healthy connection with the social and human world, he realized that he could force others at least to pay attention to him. He could elicit an actual response negatively through violence and destruction. The creature emphasized that he had, amidst his lessons with the De Lacey family, learned how to work mischief. Stealing away into a barn where a servant and lifelong friend of the Frankenstein family slept, he took the necklace of Elizabeth that William had been wearing and placed it in her pocket. He reflected that here was a lovely woman, "one of those whose joy-imparting smiles are bestowed on all but me."[27] She would suffer with this indicting evidence in her dress. The creature said, "the murder I have committed because I am forever robbed of all that she could give me, she shall atone. The crime had its source in her: be hers the punishment!"[28]

When he did finally confront his creator, the creature offered a threatening compromise—create a female companion of the same species or face systematic decimation of all whom Victor loved, of the fabric of his entire social world. The creature said of himself that he had not been destructive or violent, that the responses to him had made him so. He had concluded that "the human senses" were insurmountable barriers to any kind of union between him and another person. As a result the creature specified precisely what it was he wanted: a creature of another sex, as hideous as he; another monster that, also cut off from the world, would be all the more attached to him.

Frankenstein initially agreed, hoping to be "enfranchised from [his] miserable slavery."[29] He traveled to the remotest Orkneys of Scotland to create a laboratory in one of the three miserable huts that constituted the island when a series of concerns about bringing into being another living creature whose dispositions he could not know in advance struck him: She might, he reflected, be more malignant than her mate. She might delight in wretchedness. She "might refuse to comply with a compact made before her creation."[30] She might be repulsed and horrified by the creature's deformity and refuse him completely. Worst of all, he considered, if she did travel into obscurity with the creature, if they did "quit Europe forever" for "the most savage of places" in unknown parts of South America as the creature promised, they might have children and create a monster race.[31] Frankenstein would have been single-handedly responsible for all such disastrous outcomes, for the possibility of having authored "a race of devils [that] would be propagated upon the earth, who might make the very existence of the species of man a condition precarious and full of terror," when his only hope had been to buy his own peace, to wake from a frightful dream that had thrown him into isolation and misery that he felt he could neither explain nor share with any of the loved ones who might have offered him comfort.[32] Perhaps most lamentable were the ways in which Victor's inability or unwillingness to explain the presence of the creature had distorted all coherent understandings of responsibility and justice. Innocents had been sacrificed for deeds of which they had not even been aware. Constantly claiming that he, Victor, was the murderer of William, he still failed actually to take responsibility for his act of creation. Having usurped the role of both G-d and women in reproduction, he offered the creature neither fathering nor mothering, rendering it an orphan of a family that had prided itself in caring for children whose parents had fallen on hard times and been unable to fulfill their parental duties.

The creature, seeing Frankenstein tear the nearly complete female form to pieces, was enraged that Victor had broken his promise, allowing the creature to endure fatigue, cold, and hunger for hopes so callously destroyed. "Slave," the creature said wrathfully to Victor, "I before reasoned with you, but you have proved yourself unworthy of my condescension.... [Y]ou believe yourself miserable, but I can make you so wretched that the light of day will be hateful to you."[33] He asks why it is that Victor was to have the happiness of a wife and companions while he, the creature, was denied them. If it was all that remained, he promised, he would make Victor, his own tyrant and tormentor, miserable. The creature warned that he was fearless and therefore extremely powerful and that he would revenge the miseries that Victor had inflicted, in particular, saying that he would be present on Victor's wedding night.

After systematically murdering all of Frankenstein's loved ones and pursuing him into the Arctic north, the creature sat finally over the corpse of his creator, who had been brought aboard by Walton. The creature reflected,

[W]hile I destroyed his hopes, I did not satisfy my own desires ... still I desired love and fellowship, and I was still spurned. Was there no injustice in this? Am I to be thought the only criminal, when all human kind sinned against me? ... Nay, these are virtuous and immaculate beings! I, the miserable and the abandoned, am an abortion, to be spurned at, and kicked, and trampled on ... You hate me; but your abhorrence cannot equal that with which I regard myself.[34]

The creature swore that he would incinerate himself lest anyone encounter his horrible frame and be taken with a similar idea as was his creator. The failures of the dialectics of recognition have rarely been summed up so eloquently. Striking, too, are the theodicean dimensions of the creature's situation: his monstrosity, born first of Victor's scientific aspirations and his conception of glory, then of being so violently shunned, raise no questions about the world that has brought him into being. He alone is responsible for his monstrosity. Shelley, of course, does raise such questions, unsettling the ease with which the reader, if not the story's protagonists, designate who and what is actually monstrous.

Shelley's provocative questions about collective responsibility for the widespread destruction that followed from the excesses of Romantic conceptions of glory in the form of scientific investigation and global exploration connect richly to insights in the writings of Fanon. As Frankenstein's creature is the product of modern science, "the Negro," a major object of Fanonian investigation, is the product of modern European colonialism, of the excesses that Victor and the creature argued had characterized the shape of European encounters with the peoples of the Caribbean and South America. As Fanon reflected: "In fact, the settler is right when he speaks of knowing 'them' well. For it is the settler who has brought the native into existence and who perpetuates his existence. The settler owes the fact of his very existence, that is to say, his property, to the colonial system"[35] He reminds us, however, that the situation is not overdetermined: "It is the white man who creates the Negro. But it is the Negro who creates negritude."[36] These formulations were preceded by those in *Black Skin, White Masks*, a philosophical autobiography of the black person in an antiblack world, which was, among many other things, a meditation on the dead end of seeking recognition from those for whom one appears not as another human being but as a comparative measure of no intrinsic value. The Manicheanism of the colonial world which divides white from black ways of being, suggesting that the character of one is the enviable opposite of the other, sets up the colonized, as the creature, as the doppelganger of the colonizer. The former is the repressed and rejected side of a project that in an effort of rationalization is all that is disavowed by those who depict themselves as the legitimate standard of existence.

Parallel with *Frankenstein*, Fanon's first chapter also offers an account of searches for recognition that take linguistic form. Although more humorous, Fanon's explorations are no less tragic. In the French colonial context, Fanon explains, one is more or less civilized in direct relation to one's mastery of the continental French language. He writes, "To speak means to be in a position to use a certain syntax, to grasp the morphology of this or that language, but it means above all to assume a culture, to support the weight of a civilization."[37]

Absent in the colonial situation is a standard feature of encounters between locals and foreigners. The local, in a noncolonial context, asks visitors of their language and country. In the Antilles, in contrast, the colonized are assumed to lack both. And yet the colonized person faces a strange reality. Those black Antilleans who have mastered the French language, who can "quote Montesquieu," inspire great unease, particularly in comparison to those Martinicans to whom Frenchmen can speak down in Creole. One is reminded here of when Victor cautions Walton to be careful if the creature presents himself to the explorer when he is no longer there to intervene. Victor emphasizes, "He is eloquent and persuasive; and once his words had even power over my heart; but trust him not. His soul is hellish as his form, full of treachery and fiend-like malice."[38] Educated Martinicans, colonials similarly will warn, must be watched carefully. They appear to be "starting something," to be discontent with circumscribed roles designated for them by outsiders and to have the resources to make an argumentative case for such transgressions. They are perceived to be uppity monsters: their linguistic triumph is an anomaly. Rather than bringing them into a social world, it affirms that they are, as all monsters, without a socially acceptable place.

Another dimension of this situation manifests itself in the return of Martinicans who have traveled, at long last, to the French metropole. On their way to Europe they have studiously practiced so as not to affirm the expectation of the "reating" island men. Now back, they speak only the French equivalent of "Queen's English" (claiming to have completely forgotten their Creole), emphasizing an absolute rupture; they have avowedly returned literally new men. Fanon offers an example of a local remedy for this kind of amnesia. A peasant's son, a local boy returning home, was suffering from such a malediction, which led to his failure to identify a farm tool. The "therapy" implemented by the father was to drop the instrument on his son's foot, from which the latter screamed the identification of the tool in perfect Creole. Suggested at every turn in the French colonies is that the French language is the key that promises to open barred doors to full recognition, what comes of being able to offer technical proof of having fully imbibed a culture with genuine civilization. And yet, as with *Frankenstein,* these keys are only available if the black speaker is not seen. If and when he is, it seems the visual senses do dominate, that they are the insurmountable barriers that the creature called them. Unlike the creature, however, the colonized man who travels to "the center of the world," Paris, does already have a community of interlocutors, a sphere of intersubjective life to which he can be recalled. What the "reater" faces is a related but a different predicament. He faces the questioning of the value and degree of historicity of the world to which his language, as opposed to that of the colonizers, makes him privy, whether he can see as valuable communication with others who, like him, are perceived to be outside of fully human life. One might remember here the effort to suggest that the most innovative and cutting-edge ideas, those at the frontiers of civilization, could not be translated into rudimentary languages, or languages of communities considered "primitive."

Fanon then turns to failures to find recognition through romantic love. These searches take the outward form of black individuals seeking refuge in relationships that offer none of the affirmations that one might thereby hope for. The first story tells of Mayotte Capécia, a mixed black woman who, realizing that she cannot blacken a Manichean world divided into white and black, seeks to whiten it. She becomes a laundress and finds herself a white man, whose blue eyes, blond hair, and pale skin she loves and submits to even though she concedes that a woman of color is never completely respectable in a white man's eyes. She hopes to seal herself up in an entirely white world that will reflect back a lying image of her as also white. In the instances in which this blatantly fails, in which white women in an otherwise all-white dancehall scorn her, she blames neither them nor her lover, who says nothing, but instead blames herself and her blackness.

In the case of Jean Veneuse, a man born and orphaned in Antilles and then sent to boarding school in Bordeaux, he is supposedly European but black and therefore Negro. He spends his vacations alone at school and develops habits of solitude. He can neither assimilate nor go unnoticed. He fraternizes most easily with the dead with whom he communes through books. When white women flirt with him he warns them that it is shameful for them to associate themselves with him, who, after all, is a Negro. He wants to prove to the world that he is the equal of other men, but since only white men are ultimately men, it is he who has the profoundest of doubts. Even as he prepares to marry, he requires words of love, approval, and recognition not from his white fiancée, but from her white brother to whom he has written a letter explaining his decision to call off the engagement. The brother responds in a letter with words that acknowledge him as deserving the love not only of his fiancée but also of *a* white woman, which signifies the *any* and thus the plural *all* such women, as would a white man because he is, as the letter declares, not really black but instead "extremely brown."[39]

Finally, Fanon's narrator, as *Frankenstein's* creature, becomes the object, here *le Nègre*, which means Negro and, depending on the context, *nigger*, through an encounter with a child who, rather than being able to *see* him, responds with an extreme, caricatured version of what his parents and other adults in his world might have said of black people. Fanon's recollection is of being shattered or blown apart. He reflected that in the white world, the man of color encounters difficulty in developing his bodily schema, that consciousness of the body is a negating and a third-person consciousness, suffused with an awareness that white men have woven *le Nègre* out of details, anecdotes, and stories. The parallel with the stitching together of the creature from the parts of corpses is striking. Fanon explains that the black person faces constructing a physiological self when suddenly he hears, "Look, *un Nègre!*" an exclamation that he describes as "an external stimulus that flicked over me as I passed by," in response to which he tried to forge a tight smile. He then heard again, "Look, *un Nègre!*" "Mama, see *le Nègre*! I'm frightened!"[40] Fanon makes up his mind to laugh in response, to laugh himself into tears, but cannot. He writes, "I was responsible for my body, my face, and my ancestors. I was battered down by tom-toms, cannibalism, intellectual deficiency, fetishism, racial defects, slave ships, and above all else, above all: '*y'a bon banania!*'" (translation revised).

Dislocated, he writes, "I took myself far off from my own presence, far indeed, and made myself an object: a BLACK MAN."[41] Fanon's path to this moment parallels the creature's in many ways, but instead of resting on the frontier of modern science, his reflections are marked by its later lamentations, mediated by the emergence of natural selection in the mechanistic forces of his corporeal being and psychoanalytical explanations of the mental life. Along this path are Lacanian interpretations of recognition, marked first by a mirror stage of narcissistic development, and then the organization of power according to law as manifested in language.[42] Fanon's observations on Capécia and Veneuse followed the failure of language, which resulted in the search for self-reflection through self-deceiving forms of love. Both Capécia and Veneuse sought, in effect, *words of whiteness,* authoritative words offering their preferred image of the self. Those words, in effect, were to be mirrors, but as the mythic life of mirroring goes, as evidenced in a fairy tale such as "Snow White," forcing a mirror *to say* what one prefers does not erase the historical reality of what was seen. Recall the trauma of the mirror stage when the creature saw his reflection in the water. The experience was one of a skipped stage of development; it was his image, not the words of a child, that brought the negative realization, the explosion of the self, to him. The successive mediating stages also hold additional twists, for whereas Capécia and Veneuse sought the authoritative source of whiteness for legitimation in self-deceiving love—for them to be loved as whites—the creature at first demanded a mirror image in a female. Here, the Lacanian reading of masculinity was presaged since, in effect, the creature was demanding of his creator to fashion a woman, as G-d fashioned Eve, or perhaps Lilith, through whom he could become a man. The correlate would, in other words, be *le Nègre* seeking *la Négresse.* It is Victor's abandoning the project, in effect closing the creature's path to manhood that collapses recognition exclusively to the dialectics of the creature and him. One could argue, in other words, that this reading adds an element of a movement of missing trauma in the Fanonian narrative, namely, the rejection of *la Négresse* as woman by which *le Nègre* could emerge as man. Fanon's additional argument, however, is that such a transition could not be accounted for solely in terms of the Lacanian structural claims without recognizing the historical situation of colonization. This third term, akin to Victor's moment of dismembering the female-creature-in-the-making, suggests a similar critique of the Lacanian trope more than a century before its birth. Frustrated by the string of failures, the path into monstrosity for Fanon took the form of a plunge into Négritude, where he hoped to become *le Nègre manqué*, the Negro/Nigger gone bad, a doubling of badness because of the redundancy inherent in the formulation; the path, as with the creature, offers more failure. On one count, the failure is the relativism of a negative term. Négritude, the theory of black personality and resistance developed by the Senegalese writer Léopold Senghor and coined by the Martinican writer Aimé Césaire, was, argued Jean-Paul Sartre, only a negative term in a dialectic that could prepare blacks to enter the world stage of the universal working class.[43] "And so it is not I who make a meaning for myself," Fanon lamented, "but it is the meaning that was already there, pre-existing, waiting for me. It is not out of my bad nigger's misery, my bad nigger's teeth, my bad nigger's hunger that I will shape a torch with which to burn down the world, but it is the torch that was already there, waiting for that turn of history."[44] Fanon rightly concluded that this was something he needed not to know. In words echoing the creature's dismay at Victor's destruction of the mate from which hopes collapsed into despair, Fanon reveals in Négritude the destroyed *Négresse*: "Sartre's mistake was not only to seek the source of the source but in a certain sense to block that source."[45] Fanon's response was at first to weep, and then, recollecting himself, journey through the world of *le Nègre* and psychopathology.

Le Nègre, the creature's correlate, embraces his ability to have an effect through being violently destructive, a negative, reactionary moment. Rather than a man who occupies a political location deemed monstrous, he tries to embrace, to become the monster. Here, this monster is not a man from Martinique, a colonized island in the French Caribbean who inspired poetry, but *un Nègre*. Paget Henry explains that at the core of processes of racialization was the propagation of this caricature, "the Negro," the polar opposite of white and of normative ideals but also a fundamental disparagement of the possibility of any meaningful collective black identity or precolonial African self. For Henry, Du Bois's idea of double consciousness is a "phenomenological account of the self-consciousness of these African subjects whose 'We' had been shattered and challenged by this process of negrification," who, surrounded by projected images of the happy slave and of watermelon and fried chicken, were constantly asked what it felt like to be a problem.[46] For Fanon, *le Nègre* is the racist caricature that black people are expected to be. When they resist or fail to become this, rather than the caricature being reconsidered, there is anger at the black person for failing to be the authentic *Nègre*. In response, Fanon reflects, that he must embrace his own agency, the ability that Victor shunned in his creature, to be both "a yes" and "a no": a yes to life, love, and generosity and a no to exploitation, degradation, and butcheries of freedom. He must demand human behavior from others, without renouncing his own freedom through his own choices. He must be a black man rather than a Negro. He concludes with the interrogative of which we earlier remarked, "I want the world to recognize, with me, the open door of every consciousness. My final prayer: O my body, make of me always a man who questions!" Rather than recognize him, it is *with* him, that Fanon hopes for recognition of the openness of his own and potentially all human consciousness.[47]

It is commonly remarked that Shelley's "monster" is far better known than she is, that many more people will, upon hearing the name Frankenstein, smile in recognition, imagining a green rectangular face that produces inchoate sounds, than will recall that its creator was a young woman named Mary. Still, we think that this standard observation requires some reconsideration. Mary Shelley herself was a clear example of the very same kind of "monster" that Frankenstein's creature and Fanon's *Nègre* were and are: in her case she fatefully combined, in the nineteenth century, genius with being female. If there is any doubt, consider that she wrote a book that defined the genre of science fiction that became a gothic horror classic at the age of nineteen, while pregnant. Many might try to minimize the significance of this by emphasizing her unique parents, that she was, after all, the daughter of Mary Wollstonecraft and William Godwin. Both were famous radicals of their day. Wollstonecraft was equally revered as a pioneer feminist and writer of *A Vindication of the Rights of Woman* (1792) and denounced as a "hissing serpent" by detractors who scorned the out-of-wedlock birth of her first daughter Fanny Imlay, her two attempts at suicide, and her intellectual work that brought her into conflict with Edmund Burke.[48] She had suggested that the values of the bourgeois revolution had not completely eradicated the tyranny of privilege linked to wealth and birth rather than manifestations of reason, virtue, and exertion. Cultures of dependence remained the norm with all of the vanity, self-love, and desire for esteem that characterized them. In such worlds, women tended to be silly and base, exaggerating their dependence and weakness in the hope that they could, if appearing and adorning themselves well, become the desired object, the pretty diversion of a man. Clinging to their scepters of beauty, women cunningly manipulated men, seeking power over them since they had none over themselves. The antidote would be a society governed more rigorously by reason in which people were not led by superficial appetites that turned on deception. This would require an educational system available to all girls and boys regardless of their class that would bring them together as mundane equals who could be genuine friends rather than passionate but ultimately disillusioned and disappointed lovers.

Godwin was an "ex-Dissenting" minister and atheist who became very influential following the publication of his *Enquiry Concerning Political Justice and Its Influence on Modern Morals and Happiness* (1793). The two, in spite of their fierce criticisms of conventional marriage, wed when Wollstonecraft became pregnant. Unfortunately, she died only five months later of puerperal poisoning immediately following Mary's birth. Godwin never fully recovered. In a mournful act of devotion, he set out dutifully to recount in frank and full detail the exemplary life of his late wife.[49] Most contemporary readers did not find it cause for celebration. Although emotionally distant in ways that became even more detrimental to Mary when he remarried, Godwin assured that Mary Shelley and Fanny Imlay received the kind of progressive education for which he had argued, had access to his extensive library, and could be present as he conversed with many of the leading minds of his day, including William Wordsworth, Charles Lamb, and Samuel Taylor Coleridge. It was Godwin's early writing that attracted the interest of Percy Shelley, then a young and gifted heir who concluded that those who possessed money should give it to those who needed it most. Shelley became Godwin's benefactor and disciple until his elopement with Mary two months later.

Still, what one would conventionally expect to emerge from Mary Shelley's background would be a highly educated, worldly, and very literate young woman. She most certainly defied the bounds of the normal. Many might have seen her life as a kind of divine warning: that Shelley's mother died in childbirth, that she was born in the final years of the eighteenth century, that she eloped with a married man whose first wife consequently took her own life, that she lost three of her four children, and more generally, that she lived a life of intellectual and sexual eccentricity, may well have been taken as signs of foreboding.

In other words, we would suggest that, rather than comparing the relative renown of Shelley and her creature, we consider whether the creature, one of the prototypical monsters of the modern West, rather than what might have been its female companion, is the fruit of Shelley's own autobiographical reflections, particularly on the absence of a place for, and the seeming monstrosity of, a woman like herself.

Shelley's mother was herself fascinated by people of genius. She rejected the then "fashionable" assumption, presaging our earlier discussion of popular images of Einstein, that men of genius had delicate constitutions, reflecting that "strength of mind has, in most cases, been accompanied by superior strength of the body."[50] In her case for marriages based in friendship, "not against strong persevering passions but romantic wavering feelings," she suggested that genius writers had offered images of love that did not exist on earth. These offered excuses to people who sought a sentimental façade to what was little more than sensuality and idleness, for whom talk of virtue in long-term relationships seemed overly austere. By contrast, geniuses could "give existence to insubstantial forms, and stability to the shadowy reveries which the mind naturally falls into when realities are found vapid."[51] They would ultimately correct themselves and pay dearly for their experience, but unlike those who palely invoked them, their dreams were the product of living and lively fancy.

Mary Shelley's own unusual gifts were observed with great curiosity with her father looking for and happily greeting evidence of her greater intellectual talents than her elder sister whom he did not father. Shelley also noted that her husband, who was attracted to the idea of her as a "child of light and love," was eager that she proved herself deserving of her parentage. Mary Shelley did not write explicitly about genius, but her own novel pointedly criticized the excesses of Romantic conceptions of glory through experimental sciences and global travel conceived as the opposite of the domestic sphere and its female virtues. Victor and Walton must go off alone, away from their families and homes that they leave to the care of their sisters, and risk their own lives and endanger those of others in aspirations not envisioned by or answerable to the people left behind. Walton is able to stave off disaster by reversing course in response to considerable pressure of his crew that he is more willing to heed having witnessed the divine warning of Victor and his creature. Once begun, Victor's journey cannot end in anything but icy death.

What is more, as we hope the parallel with *Black Skin, White Masks* has suggested, Mary Shelley's reflections were not only genre-creating in the realm of horror and science fiction, but also, in a prototypical sense, in postcolonial studies. *Frankenstein* and its retelling from the point of view of both creator and created, the one refusing responsibility for what it through both action and projection brought into being, and the creature locked in a search for recognition that promises only failure, can and should be considered as a proto-postcolonial text. Why this is so requires further consideration.

Perhaps reflections concerning the possibility of birth gone terribly wrong, of creating and animating with life ill-considered aims and ideas that one cannot dispense with since they then look back at one with an independent life and will, is part of the mythic life that informs colonial endeavors that framed indigenous people as perpetually underdeveloped, whether in the form of political children in need of tutelage as subjects or as savages, even when noble. Or perhaps the prescient insight of Shelley is precisely because she so skillfully articulates what it is to be the monster by recognizing the monstrous as a social and political location, a genuinely tragic one in which the voice of the monster or the black person cannot be heard over and against its exterior form. Comparisons could be made here with Simone Weil's depiction of literary genius, which she describes as giving us "the actual density of the real." Weil writes,

> Although the works of these men [and women] are made out of words there is present in them the force of gravity which governs our souls.... In the words assembled by genius several slopes are simultaneously visible and perceptible, placed in their true relations, but the listener or reader does not descend any of them. He feels gravity in the way we feel it when we look over a precipice, if we are safe and not subject to vertigo. He perceives the unity and the diversity of its forms in this architecture of the abyss.[52]

One response to the relegation of entire categories of people—whether they be too big or too small, too bright or too dark—to the realm of the monstrous is to criticize the very idea and maintenance of a particular set of features and qualities that constitute both what is normative and normal. In their place, one might argue, must be a thorough rejection of any settled ideas about how everyone must or should be, or rather than an organizing center and core that emphasizes attributes of birth, instead stresses those of intentional agency—our actions, values, habits, and dispositions. An interesting feature of several of the constitutions written in the immediate aftermath of the Haitian Revolution was their effort to delineate requirements for citizenship that were neither racially nor ethnically based. They stressed instead one's political loyalties, commitments, and values as manifested in one's political activity and decisions concerning marriage.[53] Informing this might also be the view and corresponding warning that we all move into and out of the category of the monstrous— whether in periods of adolescence, during menstruation, or in fits of madness, for example—and that our loathing for those most tenaciously fixed in the role of monster may be colored profoundly by an effort to distance ourselves from identifications that otherwise would draw us too near. This suggestion, offered by David White, assumes that to be monstrous is to blur settled boundaries of age and generation, sickness and health, insanity and sanity. With the example of teenagers, one is really both a child and an adult and must face the quandaries of how appropriately to behave and relate both to one's parents and teachers and to one's younger siblings, relatives, or friends. In the case of menstruation, as Gloria Anzaldúa wrote in her classic *Borderlands,* one bleeds incessantly for a week but does not die.[54] One must, however comically, carry on with mundane life as if all were normal. In bouts of madness, one suddenly sees, thinks, and acts with a different orienting calculus. One indubitably makes decisions and interacts with others in ways that will look profoundly different, and often regrettable, days or hours later. As we hope such examples suggest, most human beings are episodically monstrous (in fact, there might be something monstrously inhuman about never being so) and may then look with great relief upon periods of normality. Such relief may open one up to reflection on the condition of others relegated to the category of the monstrous. It may intensify one's contempt for what is too close to home.

What seems to have emerged as a more typical though not preferable response to relegating people to the category of monsters and then blaming them for occupying that space is an attempt to refute the possibility of forging any collective set of values or purposes. This is perhaps most evident in the kind of work that dominates American political science, work that insists that all one can expect from liberal capitalist democracies and politics more generally is the aggregating of private self-interests.[55] It is as if Karl Marx and Friedrich Engels's diagnosis that self-interest and egoistic calculation would alone unite men under capitalism has become prescriptive. This most minimalist and cynical account of what it is to be a human being emphasizes our kinship to other nonhuman animals rather than stressing the unique challenges faced by the project of becoming people. This tendency manifests itself as well in metaphoric and mythic life, in the realm of the monstrous, in what we have been calling nihilistic monsters. Rather than what we might hope for through an engagement with the reflections offered by the monstrous of modernity, a kind of opening of consciousness for which Fanon argues, we find at the heart of nihilistic monsters a radical equality through which we are made most certainly equal because we have all ceased to matter.[56]

◇

4

Mute

We have thus far spoken of disaster through the concept of the sign continuum, an expressed phenomenon, and its associated string of warnings embodied, simply, as monstrosities. Warnings require their appearance. But, as we have seen, there are things whose appearance seems to be better left denied or, if emergent, restricted. How can monsters warn or manifest what they are when their ability to become symbolic has been suppressed?

Recall Homer's *Odyssey*, wherein Polyphemus, the Cyclops, entraps Odysseus and his men during their perilous journey home after the Trojan War. Polyphemus speaks. His verbosity reveals his power over his domain, which, as we saw in Euripides' interpretation, announces sodomy of his elderly male servant and his prisoner's fate as his next meal.[1] In the ancient world through much of the early modern one, whether Sphinx or Demon trickster, scientific bungle or reanimated dead, monstrous creatures presented themselves and the communities that shunned them in their own words. Frankenstein's creature, as we have seen, shined with eloquence. Mr. Hyde, Dr. Jekyll's chemically produced alter ego in Robert Louis Stevenson's *Strange Case of Dr Jekyll and Mr. Hyde* (1886), expressed his lust and anger through the medium of words. And Carmilla, as Joseph Sheridan Le Fanu's lesbian vampire in his 1872 novella bearing the villainess' name, gains her victim's trust through the seductive force of language. The list of monstrous eloquence is long. These creatures of unusual speech were, however, transformed in their most popular representations in the twentieth century—namely, cinema.[2] Monsters, at least as generally presented in film, have, until very recently, grunted.[3]

In the 1931 Hollywood interpretation of *Frankenstein*, Boris Karloff's portrayal of the creature's inner life depended more on the great actor's talent for conveying emotions with his eyes and hands. At best, the viewer received sentences without verbs of the form, "Wine, *goood!*" in between snarls. Mel Brooks brought fun to the screen in 1974 in the memorable "Puttin' on the Ritz" scene where Peter Boyle's version of the creature squeals out the song's chorus and tap dances. The humor lay in the absurdity of a linguistically-challenged monster putting on a tuxedo, dancing, and attempting to sing his way into high society. It was not until 1994, in Robert De Niro's poignant performance, that some of the Creature's speech was permitted to convey his resentment, Angst, pathos, and anger, all still with relatively few lines. Although vampires may seem to contradict this claim, we should bear in mind that vampire speech, as it were, shifts from moments of "passing" as human to those of vampiric revelation: Fangs, after all, afford little opportunity for uninflected speech.[4] And then there are zombies. Transformed from the silent enslaved figures to the mass of animated dead bodies in search of flesh, zombies exemplify the formless, material absence of clarity and distinction that, as we discussed earlier through mention of Ortega y Gasset, brings concepts and existence together in spoken ideas.

What is it that had transpired in the modern world to create speechless or linguistically challenged monsters, figures that could be dazzled by the use of signs and referents but that would ultimately remain locked outside worlds of their use? What is it about the emergence of the new millennium that is enabling such subalterns, those without the power of cultural imperialism, as they are, to speak?[5] It is our contention that this transition from speech to speechlessness and back again reflects the history of colonization and racism, which affected the political and anthropological understanding of the age. The effort to go beyond that history, to achieve a genuinely postcolonial, or perhaps simply *no longer colonial*, future has occasioned a shift from the focus on Prospero's pronouncements, the colonial protagonist of Shakespeare's *The Tempest* (c. 1610), to an effort to give voice, so to speak, to Caliban and the world he represented.[6] This consequence unleashes many forces, some of which are signs heretofore ignored but that have now returned to achieve more than being read.

An anxiety of the colonial world, one whose continued ambivalence occasions what Paul Gilroy has characterized as "postcolonial melancholia," where hegemony without formal colonies creates confused subjects, was the challenge, or threat, of the political inclusion of the colonized.[7] At the heart of this worry is the origin of the problem itself. Born from the effective dehumanization of peoples in once foreign lands, the consideration of their inclusion raises the contradictions of their original exclusion. We find here a problem of legitimation and the meaning of political life.

The legitimation problem is outlined well in a recent discussion by the famed feminist political theorist Carol Pateman.[8] Pateman provides a historically informed exploration of the "founding" narratives of three powerful modern postcolonial states—the United States, Canada, and Australia. These built their origin narrative, Pateman shows, on the notion of *terra nullius*, that is, "empty land." The contradiction of peopling empty land on which what have become known as Native Peoples lived demanded extraordinary acts of sophistry, if not imagination. The response was to make the Native Peoples themselves a site of intrinsic illegitimacy. The Native populations were expected to justify their right to their land without being able to appeal to themselves as generators of laws or sovereignty. Civilization became the criterion for the presence of people. In effect, regardless of their number, the land on which Natives lived became *terra nullius*, because such people faced an impossible criterion: They had to be other than who they were, for to be civilized was at first to domesticate land as the English in England did, then to be Christian and eventually to be European or white.[9] The outcome in the United States, Canada, and Australia is articulated well in two U.S. Supreme Court cases, *Worcester* (1831) and *Cherokee Nation v. Georgia* (1831), the latter initiated by the legal resistance of the Cherokees to their forced removal. The former announced "new and different rule" for Native Peoples in U.S. territories, and since the combination of the U.S. and Canada comprised nearly all of North America, *Cherokee* provided the conclusion of Native nations being "wards," in a "state of pupilage," of the "guardian" U.S., a view adopted also in Canada.[10] Justice John Marshall stated that rather than a "foreign state" as Cherokees claimed they were, the tribe was "peculiar," in Rogers Smith's words, "in some sense a nation [but] not fully so."[11] Pateman points out that although there is presumed rejection of any serious challenge to the basis of the three modern states established upon those original settler agreements, the empirical reality of there never really having been *terra nullius* means that the ultimate ground of their legitimacy is false. In her words:

> The logic of theories of an original contract is that the "beginning," the creation of a new civil society, is made on a clean slate. Such a

condition can be part of a thought experiment but it forms no part of the political world; the lands of the two New Worlds were not empty. *Terra nullius* is now a legally and politically bankrupt doctrine and questions about sovereignty and legitimacy will have to be tackled in the long run if a just accommodation and reconciliation is to be achieved. The three states where *terra nullius* was central to the justification of their creation pride themselves on their democratic credentials. The credentials will be more presentable once the settler contract is repudiated and a new democratic settlement is negotiated with the Native peoples.[12]

A significant feature of the postcolonies in North America and Australia (along with their "mother country" England and its correlates in Europe in relation to other postcolonies) is their influence on institutions of symbolic representation for much of the twentieth and twenty-first centuries. These countries, until very recently in the case of Australia, represent their past as one of legitimate origins. The Native populations, in such a reading, did not object to their conquest and colonization because *they could not have.* How could they have objected if they lacked civilized speech, a condition for civil society?[13] Their protestations throughout the modern era function, then, as a haunting, as a ghostlike echo of what is presumed absent as one experiences moving into an empty house with artifacts from inhabitants long gone. Their objections became audio artifacts, sounds, without decipherability in the present. Pateman challenges this assumption, pointing to the bad faith, the self-deception, involved in the construction of national ideologies that facilitate a denial of what is heard. Even if nuance is missed, a protest is an objection, a rejection of what has transpired. In this regard, her analysis, and ours, is different from the conclusion of mutedness in Gayatri Spivak's famous essay on speech and subalternality, "Can the Subaltern Speak?," for it is not that subalterns cannot speak but that they are not heard. The query poses the problem of legitimate sites of hearing, from which that activity occurs.[14] The absence of consent required more than the denial of its possibility with regard to Native Peoples; it also required its inappropriateness.

The grammar of such conquest and colonization demanded a reordered anthropology. If, for instance, the prior inhabitants are illicit, then even their appearance is a violation of things decent and good. In popular culture, this was evident in D. W. Griffith's *Birth of a Nation* (1915), where Reconstruction in the U.S. South after the Civil War is portrayed as unleashing black primitive forces embodied in a black rapist chasing a virtuous white woman to the precipice of no option but suicide. An amorous meeting of a black man and a white woman was unimaginable for those early twentieth-century audiences, and its constant reassertion as rape was indicative of a society afraid of the possibility of living otherwise. The upsurge of such forces signaled, then, violation. The film's thesis was straightforward: All Americans—white, brown, and black—were better served if political relations erected to maintain and justify the slave system were treated as the natural order, one in which whites ruled and directed while blacks, carrying out the labor this demanded, appeared only as backdrops and loyal echoes. If terrorist violence initiated by the Ku Klux Klan was necessary to restore such an arrangement, it was to be enshrined and celebrated.

The effect of colonized people as illicit appearance was, in effect, legitimation through nonappearance. It is striking, for instance, that Griffith did not hire black actors when making *Birth of a Nation*, a film that employed an incredibly large cast for its time, although there were some black people, not white actors in black face, who appeared as background and part of the landscape of some scenes. Suppression of appearance, however, was not possible on the everyday visual plane of modern life in the colonies and postcolonies since the modern world depended upon the cheap labor and enslavement of such people, which meant their constant proximity. The people who colonized them needed such people to be seen, to be marked or heard without the mediation of symbol and language. Jan Van Pieterse has demonstrated, for instance, that pictures of black slaves were not widely available in Europe until the rise of the abolitionist movement. "If slaves were depicted it was often incidentally and as part of some other subject represented. Invisibility," he writes, "was one way in which slavery was kept psychologically at bay."[15] Images chosen by abolitionist artists were carefully designed to convey that emancipation was conditional and not equivalent to an end to racism. Their central icon was, he observes, "a black kneeling, hands folded and eyes cast upward." The colonizing and enslaving groups expected the colonized and the enslaved to produce sounds without meaning, to be heard but not listened to, to become at a distance through affirming one's role as the commanded, not one who could interpret such.

Without reciprocity, without the multilateral dimensions of communication, to be communicated *to* instead of in communication *with,* these aspects of coloniality are, as Nelson Maldonado-Torres formulates them, "[modalities] of being as well as ... power relations that sustain a fundamental social and geopolitical divide between masters and slaves. Colonialism, or better put, coloniality (of power, knowledge, and being) is the spinal chord, as it were, of the modern paradigm of war."[16] As a warlike relationship, it is a collapse of speech, if by war is also understood the breakdown of communication and the commitment to and resources of non-violent efforts of resolution. As Rousseau observed in his discussion of the bellicose dimensions of enslavement: "In taking the equivalent of his life, the victor has done him no favor. Instead of killing him unprofitably he kills him usefully. Hence, far from the victor having acquired any authority over him beyond force, the state of war subsists between them just as before ... [F]ar from destroying the state of war, [enslavement] presupposes its continuation."[17] The suspension of such a relationship of violence, especially where opposition remains, in active negotiations of symbolic life and the tides of exigency, we call *politics.*[18]

As its etymology in the word *polis* reveals, politics is an activity that emerged out of the social dynamics of ancient city-states that began with the creation of a new kind of space that is fundamentally different from, and often opposed to, the open country. Walls enclosed the inner community from its outer world. As José Ortega y Gasset explains:

> [T]he Graeco-Roman decides to separate himself from the fields, from "Nature," from the geo-botanic cosmos. How is this possible? ... Where will he go, since the earth is one huge, unbounded field? Quite simple; he will mark off a portion of this field by means of walls, which set up an enclosed, finite space over against amorphous, limitless space. Here you have the public square.... [I]t is purely and simply the negation of the fields. The square, thanks to the walls that enclose it, is a portion of the countryside which turns its back on the rest, eliminates the rest and sets up in opposition to it. This lesser, rebellious field, which secedes from the limitless one, and keeps to itself, is a space *sui generis,* of the most novel kind ... an enclosure apart which is purely human, a civil space.[19]

The relationship with the limitless nature outside of the polis was primarily one of war or the threat thereof, whereas the people inside had to negotiate opposition without recourse to physical violence—behavior, in other words, that was a threat to the community. It was, in actuality, a circumstance of civility the breaking down of which constituted civil war. The former was not, however, a dainty politesse that relied upon an absence of opposition. Its significance was its ability to render apparent and withstand severe differences without the dissolution of the city-state through communication marked by its ability to effect appearance. This activity, as philosophers from Aristotle to Hannah Arendt recognized, is speech.

In speech, a subject appears to the community as a valued perspective. The speech may be challenged, but even in such instances, it could only be so by virtue of having appeared. To disagree, then, affirms that a speaker is worthy of being engaged. The "value" manifested in and by the appearance as a member of the community with the correlated set of responsibilities and potentials is understood by Aristotle as citizenship and the good life. Arendt understood the latter as glory afforded by the social world that set the conditions for and was shaped by politics. She insisted further, against nihilistic forms of equality, that the condition of politics is plurality, the fact of all human beings' similarity in our distinctiveness. If we were identical, the speech and action at the core of politics would be incoherent. It is our equality that suggests that we might reach each other through word and deed. It is our differences that make us want and need to do so.[20] More recently, and germane to our discussion, Giorgio Agamben has explored negative symbiotic oppositions through which this fragile relationship is maintained, especially in its ancient Roman example of those who have lost the legal status by which they can appear in society. As punishment, such individuals could be killed by anybody except for the sake of sacrifice, which meant, in effect, that they were rejected by society and the gods and condemned by all spheres of reality itself. Characterized as *homo sacer*, "sacred man," such an individual was outside of the law while being conditioned by it. Such a being was, in effect, no longer a man or an individual. His situation was fundamentally asymmetrical in the sense that he could be acted upon but could no longer be a source or manifestation of action. For the republican political order of which he would have been a part, he was socially, morally, and politically dead.[21]

Recalling Pateman's observations concerning how law, sovereignty, and civilization come into play in claims of *terra nullius*, the stage was set for a transformation of the symbolic structure of the condemned individual to be mapped onto the Native, whose "crime," so to speak, was of illicit occupation, of living on the land in an uncivilized manner. It is also here that we find a disruption of the sign continuum, for the status of *homo sacer* was conferred onto an individual after the warning, the crime, had shaken the community. As *ex post facto,* the symbolic grammar becomes the condition of the colonial relationship itself. Each colonized person "must be," as Sartre and Fanon observed, guilty of something since her or his continued existence is not supposed to be. The "proof" of an offense awaits its markers, its evidence. As a reinforcement of law, sovereignty, and the social borders of political life, the sign continuum from which to turn away becomes markers that link such subjects to the flawed origins of the postcolonial settler state.

We arrive, then, at the *shame,* as it were, of modern societies.[22] By shame, we mean the experience of revelation of aspects of oneself or community that one would prefer to remain hidden not only from others but also from oneself. As something of which the self would rather not be aware, shame is at home, although paradoxically uncomfortably so, in bad faith. Colonized peoples and those subject to the descent into problem people or, worse, subhuman and pariah status, the condemned and the damned, struggle to speak in communities for which their voice is marked by collective shame. For such people to speak—*really speak*—is for them to bring into the realm of appearance reminders of national or community shame, what the "we the people," to which full political membership refers, would rather leave unsaid. Consider Anna Julia Cooper's reflections on this situation, on what she argued the "American conscience would like ... from the black man's ghost":

> It is no fault of the Negro that he stands in the United States of America today as the passive and silent rebuke to the Nation's Christianity, the great gulf between its professions and its practices, furnishing the chief ethical element in its politics, constantly pointing with dumb but inexorable fingers to those ideals of our civilization which embody the Nation's highest, truest, and best thought, its noblest and grandest purposes and aspirations.[23]

The response of the nation or community is often defensive: Such people, colonized and racially inferior people, as Fanon quipped, are always starting something; they jeopardize the sense of national, communal wholeness. Usually framed as tenaciously strong, the nation's fragility is revealed by such utterances. It is no accident that worries of "divisiveness" usually accompany any national effort to discuss colonization, enslavement, or racism. It is frequently suggested that actually engaging these themes and their histories in countries such as Australia, Brazil, Canada, and the United States, among many others, is literally too much to bear, that the "we," as the people of these nations know themselves as a nation, could not survive such frank talk. Such a fear appeals to a prior innocent condition of wholeness.

The monster, as we have been arguing, is a warning. What the monster is read as a warning against, however, affects the rallying forces of society. The construction of Native, colonized, and racialized people as monsters reflects something gone wrong in the unifying narrative of the countries that produce them as such. Refusal to admit a history of foundations manqué, bad origins, leads to a theodicy of the nation, where all things bad, unjust, and evil are pushed, through the rationalizations of institutions and national ideology, outside of the social world in a perverse structure of belonging only as external beings, as the damned caught in a living hell in which their suffering cannot be transmuted in this life as historically significant or as sacrifice to the divine.[24] Such outsiders enable an affirmation of national goodness, justice, and even holiness because of the delusional assertion of completeness or maximal consistency at systemic and metasystemic levels.[25]

The expectation of having silent, dehumanized subjects is, however, insufficient for the maintenance of national bad faith. Silence is disturbingly neutral, ultimately revealing neither approbation nor dissent, although where power relations are radically asymmetrical, it is a recognition of the irrelevance of one's thoughts, especially those made manifest in one's words. The dominating group thus *needs* the dominated to say something, but since the conditions of such utterance are already poisoned by the structure of self-denial, speech is not what emerges. Instead, other forms of expression surface—those saturated by emotion and others blocked by inscrutability.[26] From the end of the nineteenth century and throughout the twentieth, this need has been a demand from which a steady supply of art has enriched modern life. In addition to their many existential insights, what has been the impetus of Negro Spirituals, the blues, and the many popular developments from rhythm and blues and rock 'n' roll to hip hop, and the grumblings made into a roar in subaltern literatures, but for the misery beneath the repressed depths of the modern, and for many, postmodern soul?[27] Recall here Søren Kierkegaard's response to the question "What is a poet?," his own description of the transmutation of suffering through political impotence into song. He writes:

> An unhappy man who in his heart harbors a deep anguish, but whose lips are so fashioned that the moans and cries which pass over them are transformed into ravishing music. His fate is like that of the unfortunate victims whom the tyrant Phalaris imprisoned in a brazen bull, and slowly tortured over a steady fire; their cries could not reach the tyrant's ears so as to strike terror into his heart; when they reached his ears they sounded like sweet music. And men crowd about the poet and say to him, "Sing for us soon again"—which is as much as to say, "May new sufferings torment your soul, but may your lips be fashioned as before; for the cries would only distress us, but the music, the music is delightful."[28]

Aside from the joys of entertainment, a perverse development has been a form of competition for the performance of such artistic expression. In antiblack societies, there is a long history of non-black performance of darkness. Blackface is a familiar example, but at the level of mundane life, black popular culture has been the leitmotif of white reverie. The historian Michael Alexander offers a fascinating exploration of this phenomenon.[29] In an attempt to explain the behavior of European Jews who came of age in the America of the 1920s, he asks why it is that an upwardly mobile group that was not alienated in political, economic, and social terms continued, in large numbers, to identify themselves with people who remained on the actual margins. Some of those Jews did this by participating in political groups that made collaborators of more marginal Americans. Others used their relative leverage in public life to defend the marginal. Others still, in particular Al Johlson, imitated them. Alexander explains that it was typical of the time for comedians to play characters that belonged to their own ethnic group, and yet there was a spate of Jews who donned blackface, claiming, in each instance, that their doing so had initially been an accident, that their minstrelsy had been "naturally inspired."[30] Indeed, blackface had gone considerably out of style, as it was associated in the Northern United States with nineteenth-century race politics. Its resurgence was due to the work of "white" Jewish agents and "white" Jewish performers singing songs by Jews in plays written by Jews.[31] Alexander rejects the more standard explanations that would argue that by so ineffectively pretending to be blacks, those Jews were, in fact, trying to whiten themselves. Alexander insists that this cannot explain why it was that a man like Johlson donned blackface night after night in thousands of performances. No, this was evidence of a desire of such performers to be their own construction of blackness.[32] Euro-American Jews, Alexander concludes, constructed "an elaborate vision of American blackness, nearly irrespective of actual African Americans or African-American culture, and then attempted to embody that vision."[33] But more, Alexander suggests, drawing on the work of Johan Huizinga, this representation was identification. "The effect," he writes, "is not so much shown figuratively as actually reproduced in action."[34] For Eastern European Jews who understood themselves in terms of social alienation and exile, this was an expression of an effort to find a way to be Jews in the United States. For them the "Jewish imagination of African-American culture was an empty set, a longing to incorporate that which was never really considered but only imagined."[35] Such an account suggests a very different way of interpreting at least some dimensions of what has been dubbed the ongoing Black–Jewish conflict in the 1960s and subsequently.[36] What would emerge when Johlson had actual contact with a black person and one who did not exhibit the qualities and character that he had projected onto blackness? Would Johlson feel threatened in his monopoly on the theatrical interpretation of what it meant to be authentically black? Would he resent people who actually occupied the social location to which his own interpretations referred? Several recent autobiographies by vocal Jewish neoconservatives suggest that the answer to the final question is a definitive "yes."

This form of exoticism, of the dominant and those seeking membership among the dominant groups temporarily taking on and playing versions of the dominated, is a recurring theme across the globe well into the present. One need simply look at the popular cultural superstars playing Native and playing black in a variety of entertainment media from South Africa, Australia, and the United States to see our point. The joy of participation in varieties of world music and forms of dance is not in itself bad, and it is not always a case of what has become known as "cultural appropriation," though one is immediately struck by the complete (and seemingly uncharacteristic) abandon with which many whites throw themselves into such a rendezvous with darkness. Whether blues, jazz, rhythm and blues, or hip-hop, these musical forms in the United States are, after all, indigenous to that country. A white Americans enjoying and performing such music is, in other words, simply involved in the creolized popular culture of her or his country, one in which, as we and many others have pointed out, political expression often took artistic form in the absence of other institutional avenues. For some, however, the goal is not simply to participate but to outperform the dominated subjects at the aesthetic expression of their situation. The result is a fictional form of authenticity, one of the fantasy of mastery by consent of the dominated.[37] For the white in cultural blackface, this means being more authentically black than blacks. The "whigger" ("white nigger") is one example, but, as many blacks in Black Studies can attest, there is no shortage of white scholars and students who assert claims to having greater knowledge, even of the existential dynamics, of black life or the performance of black aesthetic practices than their black counterparts.[38] This is not to discount the value of academic knowledge or artistic talent. Our point is about the need reflected by such assertions, a need, literally, to have it all. They suggest another dimension of national shame—greed—to which we will return in the next chapter.

Alleviating the causes of national shame demands the responsibility of the dispossessed, dominated, and oppressed for their situation. There is thus a national need for the avowed faults of such people to be made manifest in their actions. A double condemnation emerges in exoticizing performances. In playing dark, so to speak, members of the dominant group deceive themselves with the belief that they could be a better version of those whom they imitate. In effect, in the case of antiblack racism, the nation needs blacks to fail not only at being what they are not (whites and other nonblacks) but also at being what they are (blacks). Léopold Senghor and Frantz Fanon, among others, have noted the ways in which the Manichaenism of colonialism seeks to divide up human characteristics and abilities racially. For Senghor this clearly illustrated the need of European values for the complementary contributions of other races and continents to revitalize and fertilize them. Our point here is that "the whigger" is not content with being able to claim the attributes designated white—rationality, intelligence, innovation, order; he or she must have those of Négritude—soul, emotion, musicality, eros—as well. In the genre of autobiography, there are countless examples across political spectra, from neoconservative to progressives and even Marxists, of a strange envy of blacks to the point that such whites even rationalize themselves as victims of black having an undeserved privilege of blackness.[39] Encounters with blacks who can "out-black them," so to speak, trigger a form of narcissistic rage in such exoticists.[40] For such individuals, black cultural expression, even black speech, can only be legitimate if it needs, or can only emerge through, their mediation. It becomes the absence by which their necessity, as purveyors of presence, is affirmed.

Yet, as we have been arguing, sign continua are never permanent. The extent to which members of a society are willing to respond to their warnings will determine effects of what falls from even imagined heavens. In popular culture, some monsters have become sexy. In vampire lore, for instance, such creatures have become objects of desire and even desirable. As audience identification increases, whether for those in the Hollywood films *Blade* (1998, with sequels and a television series), *Twilight* (2008 movie, novel 2006), or the *HBO* series *Trueblood* (2008, based on the novel *Dead Until Dark*, 2001) and many more, a split has occurred in which there is the monster among other monsters, an often mixed figure (more human with vestiges of monstrosity) who, reminiscent of tragic mulattos of race narratives, speaks through struggles of purification: In their struggle against the *real monsters*, they are allies of established orders of right and good. Speech is afforded to them, these mediating exemplars of divine warning, through the limited speech of the monsters against which they fight. In one instance, the exemplar is the information gained from the suffering voice of tortured bodies, which identifies the whereabouts or activities of other monsters. In another instance, this narrative eerily maps on to recent, hybrid exemplars of race mediation in postcolonies. Monsters, in other words, can speak if and only if it is against other monsters.

"Lawfare can be limited or it can reduce people to 'bare life,'" write Jean Comaroff and John Comaroff.[41] They continue: "But ultimately, it is neither the weak nor the meek nor the marginal who predominate in such things. It is those equipped to play most potently inside the dialectic of law and disorder. This ... returns to ... the notion that the law originates in violence and lives by violent means, the notion, in other words, that the legal and the lethal animate and inhabit one another. Whatever the truth of the matter, politics at large, and the politics of coercion in particular, appear ever more to be turning into lawfare." Although writing of the postcolony in the early years of the new millennium, the Comaroffs' observation recalls our earlier discussion of monstrosity, where the monster is a being on which all is permitted as a matter of the reconstitution of order. The violent underpinnings of many legal systems need not be ashamed of themselves when unleashed against the monster, as seen in, for example, the methodical sadism of the Inquisition as Christendom, having officially extricated the Moors and Jews from Spain, sought to find those Jews and Moors hidden within the newly converted populations that remained. In addition to cries of suffering, torture forced words from the body of the accused and the condemned, confessions of monsters lurking within their bodies and pointing to those hidden throughout Christian communities in Iberia and its extensions in the New World. In the wake of slave revolts in the Americas, torture demanded similar words from the enslaved in an effort to suppress those rebellions and to prevent future ones. In the Holocaust, torture was used to root out blacks, communists, Gypsies, homosexuals, and most infamously Jews. Torture in these instances is facilitated by practices of dehumanization, where the tortured becomes a thing on which to act and the torturer a mechanism of interrogation. Throughout this collapse into the mode of being things are human beings hidden by the cloak of ideological rationalizations. As Peter Caws observes:

> One convenient way of escaping responsibility for unfortunate social facts (private property and wage labor, for example) is to regard them as relations between people and things: The capitalist is related to his property, so the expropriated worker vanishes from the equation; the worker is related to his work, so the factory owner similarly vanishes. Marx insists that both are disguised relations between people and other people: The owner of private property deprives, and the wage slave is enslaved to, human beings in flesh and blood, not economic abstractions.[42]

In many societies, torture is among the "unfortunate social facts" of which Caws speaks. Government police and soldiers routinely seek out people whose status is that of a thing whose suffering is permissible and tolerable for the edifying purpose of their elimination and for the reconstitution of threatened state power.

According to Elaine Scarry, torturers, through inflicting intense physical pain while demanding answers of the tortured, aim to confer on themselves and those for whom they work the qualities of extreme bodily suffering that they elicit, in particular "its incontestable reality, its totality, its ability to eclipse all else, its power of dramatic alteration and world dissolution."[43] The increasingly violent methods of interrogation supposedly required to coerce urgently needed information from the tortured through turning everything in the physical environment—from accoutrements of mundane civilization to the tortured's own body—into weapons engulf the interrogated in a suffering that is so total that it is world-dissolving. "It is the intense pain that destroys a person's self and world," Scarry explains, "a destruction experienced spatially as either the contraction of the universe down to the immediate vicinity of the body or as the body swelling to fill the entire universe. Intense pain is also language-destroying: as the content of one's world disintegrates, so the content of one's language disintegrates; as the self disintegrates, so that which would express and project the self is robbed of its source and its subject."[44] The world of the tortured shrinks into less than the confines of his body as the territory of the torturer expands. The torturer in "the interrogatory, the declarative, [and] the imperative" becomes a colossal voice without a body as the tortured, though uttering sounds, collapses into a body with no voice.[45] In torture, Scarry concludes, "one person gains more and more world-ground not in spite of but because of the other's sentience: the overall equality it works to bring about, 'the larger the prisoner's pain, the larger the torturer's power' can be restated, 'the more sentient the prisoner, the more numerous and extensive the torturer's objects of sentience. The middle steps in the equation can also be rewritten in this language: to say ... 'the torturer uses the prisoner's aliveness to crush the things that he lives for.'"[46]

Torture continues to be an element of dealing with national monsters. The War on Terror initiated by the attacks on the Twin Towers and the Pentagon Building in the United States on September 11, 2001, led to one of the more shameful chapters of recent American history—namely, Abu Ghraib Prison in Iraq and the Camp Delta in Guantánamo Bay, Cuba, among many others secretly spread across the globe. Agamben's discussion of the state of exception recurs in many analyses of this development, as Joshua Comaroff points out, since the circumstances of national security from the threat of terrorism was advanced by President George W. Bush to legitimate the absence of limits available for the seizure of individuals who were then interrogated in these facilities; law, in other words, was being suspended for the apparent sake of protecting law or at least a supposedly law-abiding world. "Camp Delta is an analogue, here," Comaroff observes, however, "of Auschwitz, in kind if not degree: it is a nonjuridical space wherein unmediated power is exerted over captives."[47] Yet, argues Comaroff, what is overlooked in an appeal to Agamben (and Carl Schmitt) in this context is that the suspension of law has never really been a necessary condition for state violence in the United States and many other countries: "Agamben elides such mundanities with the most spectacular of instances, regardless of the specificities of difference. In the timeless vacuum of *homo sacer*, the eternal truth of sovereignty is a brutal seizure of the political life of the populace.... More important, however, is the question of whether exception is necessary for the exercise of repressive force.... Its suspension is hardly required for repressive acts to occur, hence the revelation, post-Abu Ghraib, that the famous torture techniques were imported, at least in part, from the American prison system. What seemed grotesque and exceptional was actually standard operating procedure, common practice, and de facto legal—all of which raises some profound concerns about the usefulness of this theory."[48] Although Comaroff devotes the rest of his analysis to the exploration of how a sociogeopolitical analysis would reveal how the logic of geography, in this case the semiotics of islands as places of control (think of how many famous prisons as well as utopias were islands) are in stream with legal rationalities of operationalized violence, his criticisms echo an observation by Aimé Césaire in the 1950s, since the overwhelming demographic of populations subject to legalized violence in the modern world are people of color: Hitlerism, Césaire argued, was not an aberration, a state of exception, but an ordinary feature of colonial practices brought to their center. European colonialism only considered its practices barbaric, he argued, when applied against (white) Europeans. Thus, from Césaire's point of view, European outrage at the Holocaust against European Jews was not in fact an argument against genocide and brutal exploitation but over *whom* such activities should be committed against. There was, in other words, never a denial of the acceptability of violence but of the legitimacy of violence when applied to certain populations. Such practices were mundane features of life in the colonies and against blacks (and, although he does not mention them, Native American populations). This is because of the philosophical anthropology of dehumanization that governed everyday life under such a system:

> colonization ... dehumanizes even the most civilized man; that colonial activity, colonial enterprise, colonial conquest, which is based on contempt for the native and justified by that contempt, inevitably tends to change him who undertakes it; that the colonizer,

who in order to ease his conscience gets into the habit of seeing the other man as *an animal*, accustoms himself to treating him like an animal, and tends objectively to transform *himself* into an animal.[49]

Jean and John Comaroff's examination of the continuation of such practices brings to the fore the global dimension of operationalized violence through the fetishization of legal relationships, and although the tortured, as Joshua Comaroff has argued, is locked in a geopolitics, a social geography, of "a space of contradictions," we should remember that the avowed purpose of those contradictions is for a resolution of what undergirds all legalized violence—namely, continued social welfare.[50] It is for the sake of the community, whose idealized chimera is the self-referential "us," that information is sought. The tortured detainees are not, in popular imagination, *anybody*; they are, in their symbolic form, bodies in the way of themselves, signs beneath which are other signs, which makes them doors blocking access to the flow of signification. But as such signifiers, they stimulate a doubled movement of warnings, for the torturer also emerges as a monster when "discovered" by a society appealing to claims of nonviolent authority. In effect, the torturer's moral status becomes a warning initiated by the monster tortured, but then a new chain of significations of recovery begin; shame, in other words, becomes the turning away from that dimension of law, and a reassertion of the nation's eating its cake and having it, too, comes to the fore. The monster does not here speak, but the monster's suffering points to sites of threats to the legal order, namely, other monsters. When all is permitted against the threat to the nation, it could only be so if the nation lacks fault or responsibility for the emergence of its enemy. There is, then, a failure to take heed of what the emergence of the monster and other monsters signify, so the chains of sign continua, although forced to cry out and locate their continuation, lack a political voice, and therefore do not properly speak, but are with a consequence of tension between the political and the legal. As Joshua Comaroff concludes: "if we are to pay heed to the ongoing debates about the legality and efficacy of torture—it creates the very intelligence it was designated to extract, and the kind of enemy against which it defines its present and future."[51]

In recent history, the mediating voice of hybridity speaks out against the nation's monsters as a moral voice, although paradoxically in the form of a reasserted purity since the polar extremes, of, for example, white and black, are affirmed, with brown through beige governed by a logic of distance from the latter and closeness to the former. Booker T. Washington was an endeared figure in white America from his famous Atlanta Comprise speech in which he compared segregating the races to separate fingers belonging to the same hand.[52] Martin Luther King Jr. marked an important, radical shift from the Washington model and offered a messianic assertion of moral will and courage over state implements of violence. His rhetorical power as a moral voice reverberated beyond the shores of his native land as his being awarded the Nobel Peace Prize attested. Corey D. B. Walker, commenting on King's famous "I Have a Dream" speech, observes:

> Staged with the backdrop of the Lincoln Memorial and witnessed by thousands[53] of Americans seeking to instantiate the social and political rights of African Americans, King's speech resolutely articulates the promises and perils of the democratic experience in the United States. King fabricates an extensive rhetorical architecture in order to conceptualize the conflicted and contested political space in the United States while gesturing toward a new model of democratic existence whereby all national subjects will have the opportunity to freely and fully engage in political life. King's strategic use and deployment of the construct of the "dream" signifies on the national symbolic, particularly as captured by the idea of "the American Dream," while carving out a new space for a more robust articulation of political presence and possibility of African American civic and political equality. "Now is the time to make real the promises of democracy," King emphatically announces. Overlapping the particular with the universal, the social with the economic, as well as the moral with the political enables King to develop a series of critical points of reference whereby the struggles and conflicts, the possible resolution and enhancement of American democracy can become tangible in the lives of the marginal and dispossessed.[54]

Yet, in spite of King's efforts to make clear the *political* significance of his thought, which played no small role in his assassination, it is the model of him as a pre-political figure, as one struggling in spite of politics instead of by way of it, which dominates the American national memory. King, as a symbol of the moral character and unity of the United States, its primary spokesman on nonviolence, became frozen in the mediating trope of a more innocent Civil Rights Movement that supposedly became adulterated by a more divisive and violent Black Power movement.[55] The counterposed, feared genealogy of W.E.B. Du Bois and Paul

Robeson, voices of protest and patently political speech, has heirs who ironically include Martin Luther King Jr. and Malcolm X. All four suffered surveillance and reprisal from the U.S. government and hostility from the American public as their words increasingly transformed from a moralistic voice to political dissent, in a word, *speech.* Du Bois was arrested, and although exonerated, ultimately went into exile. Robeson's passport was revoked, and venues through which he could make a living dried up from state pressure. For an international figure of his stature, confinement to the U.S. was tantamount to life in prison.[56] An ironic feature of the transformation from the times of high colonialism and the Cold War to more recent times is the use of Robeson's performance of Negro Spirituals as one of the leitmotifs of the path of Senator Obama to the U.S. Presidency and his place in history as the first black person to win that post. King and Malcolm X were assassinated, but how they are remembered is entirely a function of the inclusion of the former and the continued fear of and ambivalence toward, if not exclusion, of the latter. Malcolm X anticipated this when near the end of his life he commented:

> You watch. I will be labeled as, at best, an "irresponsible" black man. I have always felt about this accusation that the black "leader" whom white men consider to be "responsible" is invariably the "black leader" who never gets any results … I have been more reassured each time the white man resisted me, or attacked me harder—because each time made me more certain that I was on the right track.[57]

The Martin Luther King Jr. for whom there is a national holiday in the United States is categorically the one of a triumphant moral symbol and nonviolence. Although King was an advocate of nonviolent resistance, developed from his relationship with the Quaker existential philosopher and theologian Howard Thurman and their time with Mahatma Ghandi in India, what is misleading in this ascription is the reality faced by blacks in struggles against antiblack racism: the history of racial violence in the United States was not by blacks on whites as a group but by the latter, often in large mobs, on blacks.[58] In effect, nonviolence was being demanded of blacks against, as Malcolm X argued, their acting in *self-defense.* Blacks, in other words, were being asked not to defend themselves. King argued that bringing the moral ugliness of antiblack racism out in the open was a form of defense, at least as he understood nonviolent resistance. What was overlooked, however, is what Fanon argued in his discussion of violence in *Les Damnés de la terre*: violence could only be seen as such when its victims' humanity is recognized.[59] Without that, nearly all is permitted against them, and it is their efforts at protecting themselves and asserting their humanity that would be regarded as violent because presumed illicit. That meant that however brutal whites were, they did not consider their actions as violent so long as they were against blacks. The American white majority only saw violence when blacks fought back. This aspect of King's legacy exemplifies Malcolm X's fears of appeasement, for if blacks fighting in self-defense were monstrous, how could justice for black people ever be achieved?[60]

The significance of King's political message, of his resolute anti-imperialism, his critique of capitalism, and the more liberatory dimensions of his theology place him, however, more in stream with Reverend Jeremiah Wright, the controversial minister from whom Barack Obama was compelled to distance himself during his run for the presidency. "A More Perfect Union," Obama's famed March 2008 speech on race, was at first an effort to allay the fears of American whites of his proximity to and sympathies with black nationalism or any other black politics that they perceived to be angry, radical, and particular, but it was also his effort to negotiate the proverbial elephant in the room, given his own racial background as the offspring of a black Kenyan man and a white Irish-American woman.[61] In it, he depicted an America that had required political struggle to bridge the divide between its highest ideals and historical practices and insisted that progress in this direction required affirming common hopes and a desire for unity that transcended "a purely racial lens." Although there had been racial talk about Obama being "too black" or "not black enough," Wright, Obama argued, had introduced a level of racial divisiveness that was dangerous. He said of his pastor's sermons and speeches, "They weren't simply a religious leader's effort to speak out against perceived injustice. Instead, they expressed a profoundly distorted view of this country—a view that sees white racism as endemic, and that elevates what is wrong with America above all that we know is right with America." Obama attempted to distinguish Wright's moral from political purchase and to emphasize his own relationship to the former—that it was Wright who had brought Obama into Christianity and kindled in him a sense of hope linked to its moral mission of love and care.[62] Obama tried delicately to offer a way to talk about race that could be framed neither as evasive nor as despairing. Wright had erred toward the latter, suggesting that the United States is a place in which Obama could not enunciate cause for black anger or speak politically and be elected. Obama offered his own biography and potential victory as a uniquely American triumph that the citizenry alone could together bring into being.

Our theme about hybridity came to the fore in that speech, where Obama's legitimacy depended upon making clear the distance he was willing to forge from black divine warnings.[63] We should like to add here that hybridity, as we are using it, does not necessarily refer to racial mixture, although in the case of Obama it clearly does. Even if there were a black presidential candidate who was not an offspring of a white parent and a black one, the challenge of being tugged by a black America and the rest of the country would be there. Obama argued that this tugging was itself a political failure that he hoped finally to move the nation beyond. Although Booker T. Washington was racially mixed, the times in which he lived were such that that dimension of his identity was nearly never acknowledged. The hybridity to which he had to appeal, as did Obama, is connected to a structure that renders blackness particular and gradations through to whiteness more universal. It is, in other words, to the universal where the call of hybridity beckoned. That Obama differentiated himself from the radicality of a liberation theological call of justice, one that emanates from an absolute singularity (G-d) as a viewpoint of disclosure that would occasion national shame, brings to the fore an insight from Søren Kierkegaard: the universal is an attempt to domesticate two transcending terms—the Absolute and the individual.[64] Obama emerged as an exception that affirmed the secularized theodicean rule: America works.

The logic of exception by which the rule stays intact results in an almost perverse feature of American antiblack racism: Contemporary racism requires a loved absence by which a hated presence is maintained. Put differently, in addition to the negative image of black people that many non-blacks may have is a sometimes secretly harbored, idealized image of the exception, of a perfect black individual whom they could love, admire, even idolize. In its structure, it props up the antiblack racist into the presumed standpoint of legitimate judgment of who, among all the black people in the world, counts as worthy. In their opinion editorial for *The New York Times* on the eve of the 2009 Presidential Inauguration, Henry Louis Gates Jr. and John Stauffer observed that even the much-venerated President Lincoln, after whom Obama was making sure to evoke as many correlations with himself as possible, worked within this logic of idealized exception:

> As president, [Lincoln] became quite taken with one black man, Frederick Douglass, who initially seems to bear much in common with Barack Obama. Both Mr. Obama and Douglass had one black and one white parent; both rose from humble origins to become famous before age 45; both are among the greatest writers and orators of their generations; and both learned early to use words as powerful weapons. Lincoln, seeing this masterly orator of mixed-race ancestry, would most likely first have been reminded of his exceptional friend, Douglass.
>
> Lincoln's respect for Douglass—the first, and perhaps only, black man he treated as an intellectual equal—was total. He met with him at the White House three times and once told a colleague that he considered Douglass among the nation's "most meritorious men." And just after delivering his second inaugural address, Lincoln asked Douglass what he thought of the speech, adding that "there is no man in the country whose opinion I value more than yours."[65]

The power of the idealized exception is such that it stimulates devotion, even obsession, because of its symbolic potency: It is a function of its expected impossibility. Because once deemed impossible, because ideal, it arrives as a magical or divine force, for only magicians, gods, or G-d can achieve the impossible. Writing on magic, Richard Cavendish explains:

> Against this background, the simplest reason for believing in magic is that it works: not always, but often enough to inspire confidence. The Nile normally does flood, the rains usually do fall. And confidence in magic can cause it to work. When a spell is cast to heal someone who is sick, and he believes in it, his belief may help him to recover. When a spell is cast to murder a man, and he believes in it, his belief may kill him. A case was reported from Australia a few years ago of an aborigine [sic] who was dying, though there was nothing physically wrong with him, because he knew that a medicine-man had put a death spell on him. When he was taken to hospital and placed in an iron lung, he became convinced that this magic was stronger than the medicine-man's and he recovered. Because of this psychological mechanism, belief in magic helps to bind the members of a community together and give them strength, not merely by warding off supernatural evil which they fear but by inspiring positive confidence.[66]

The mythic power of a living, idealized object magically draws upon hidden resources in the individual who encounters it, as attested to by the multitudes, 2,000,000 in number, who gathered at the presidential inauguration of Barack Obama on that cold Tuesday morning, facing threat of hyperthermia, in an act of devotion, reminiscent of the multitudes who gathered for the Sermon on the Mount from a distant age, to the embodiment of what they thought they would never see. As commentators pondered the supposed changed discourse on race in the nation that was felt around the world, many failed to see how actually consistent the whole phenomenon was with the nation's racial logic: who, in the end, of *any racial background,* could stand as a genuine equal to a political genius offered as the basis of eradicated excuses? Obama's predecessor, an ardent opponent of affirmative action, could not match the talent and intellect of even some of the weakest members of Obama's team, and unlike Obama, whose spellbound audience were drawn by the power of his words and the belief in him as an ideal exception—what, in other words, Hannah Arendt calls *power*—his predecessor depended on force, coercion, and the promise of security through the perpetuation of a constant state of insecurity.[67]

President Obama, as the chief executive of the United States, also represents the nation and thus embodies its hopes and its ideals. In this regard, there is a subtext of the unleashed symbolic forces in the moralism exemplified by the additional element of Obama's racial designation as the first *black* president. Recall Sara Ahmed's observation of shame as an exposure of the failed self before an ideal. This ideal brings the ideal self to the fore. Her reflection on such an ideal affirms some of our thoughts on love and the perfect exception:

> The 'ideal self' does not necessarily have certain characteristics; the 'content' of the ideal is in some sense empty. Idealisation, which creates the effect of an ideal, is contingent because it is dependent on the values that are 'given to' subjects through their encounters with others. It is the gift of the ideal rather than the content of the ideal that matters. Such an 'ideal' is what sticks subjects together (coherence); through love, which involves the desire to be 'like' an other, as well as to be recognized by an other, an ideal self is produced as an approximation of the other's being. Through love, an ideal self is produced as a self that belongs to a community; the ideal is a proximate 'we'. If we feel shame, *we feel shame because we have failed to approximate 'an idea' that has been given to us*

through the practice of love. What is exposed in shame is the failure of love, as a failure that in turn exposes or shows our love.[68]

On a national level, what is sought through the exposure of shame under the weight of such an ideal is national recovery. "The nation," Ahmed writes, "is reproduced through expressions of shame in at least two ways. First, shame may be 'brought onto' the nation by illegitimate others (who fail to reproduce its form, or even its offspring), such as queer others, or asylum seekers. Such others are shaming by proxy: they do not approximate the form of the good citizen. As citizens, they are shaming and unreproductive: they cannot reproduce the national ideal. Second, the nation may bring shame 'on itself' by its treatment of others; for example, it may be exposed as 'failing' a multicultural ideal in perpetuating forms of racism."[69] The nation reconstitutes itself in shame, however, by insisting through shame that its failure is *temporary: "By witnessing what is shameful about the past, the nation can 'live up to' the ideals that secure its identity or being in the present.* In other words, our shame *means that we mean well,* and can work to reproduce the nation as an ideal."[70] This payoff of shame is, however, deceptive: "It exposes the nation, and what it has covered over and covered up in its pride in itself, but at he same time *it involves a narrative of recovery as the re-covering of the nation."*[71] The symbolic rationalization offered by Obama is that the nation's shamefully racist behavior was only temporary, and in the admission of shame will be the recovery of the nation, whose ideals, as he spelled them out in his inauguration speech, are ideal and thus transcend the nation's shame. The nation, in other words, in shame, ultimately does not have to change itself because it has expressed its deeper ideal. In Obama, the nation receives the reflection of itself that it prefers. Such mirroring is seductive, and many have been seduced, because it is, as we have observed, an ideal with which it is difficult not to fall in love, and, as Ahmed argues, it is a gift, a gift of the ideal self. In this regard, everyone, including antiblack racists, has good reason to love Obama.

In political terms, Ahmed's analysis raises an interesting problem for the nation's effusion of love for President Obama. She writes:

> An expression of shame can be a substitute for an apology, while an apology can be a substitute for shame. The expression of shame is a political action, which is not yet finished, as it depends on how it is 'taken up'. Shame, in other words, does not require responsible

action, but it also does not prevent it. Indeed, the risk of shame for the nation may be that it *can* do too much work in the uncertainty of the work that it is doing. It is no accident that public expressions of shame try to 'finish' the speech act by converting shame to pride.... The affective economies at work, ... they re-cover the national subject, and allow recovery for 'civil society', by allowing the endless deferral of responsibility for injustice in the present.[72]

The logic behind Ahmed's observations come to the fore in an imagined scenario of an enactment of reparations for enslavement of Africans and genocidal efforts against Native Americans coming from a *black* president. Although it is the office that is supposed to embody the act, is that an act that works as one of recovery if initiated by a black body?

Within the logic of American antiblack racism, other constants remain. The love Barack Obama and Michelle Obama displayed under the public eye beguiled the nation, perhaps the world, but it would have been a liability or, even worse, would have made his candidacy stillborn if Michelle Obama were white. A subtext of public affection never before seen by a presidential candidate or president is its power to put at rest a lurking fear with echoes from *Birth of a Nation*: at least this exceptional black man's eyes and heart were not focused on white women, even though his deceased mother was white. At the level of symbol, where many men seek some dimension of their mother in their wives, as many wives who love their fathers do in their husbands, this exceptional black man would have been jeopardized by such a choice. This is not to argue that the Obama family's love is not genuine. Our point is about the grammar of how such magic works in a nation with the racially infused logic of the United States. His choices, from his religion to his spouse, did not challenge the nation's most sacred mythic moorings. Among these was, as well, the symbolic summoning of Abraham Lincoln, the nation's great emancipator, savior-leader of the union, and martyr. As rituals of channeling Lincoln, from that nineteenth-century senator from Illinois to this twenty-first century senator from Illinois, took shape in a convergence of hands on the same Bible, the symbolic structure of affirmed whiteness and denied blackness continued through the absence of the nineteenth-century symbolic structure of hybridity in Frederick Douglass (white master father, black enslaved mother) and his relation to the abolitionist movement on the one hand, and the late twentieth-century correlate of rising to the leadership of the racist, or at least believed to be no longer racist, state: Nelson

Mandela. The inauguration's rituals of symbols called for the idealized exception to signal evocations of ruling whiteness with other black signifiers as suppressed terms.

To his credit, Obama commenced a program of political and ethical rectification from the moment his presidency was made official. He announced and set up a group of advisors to close the Guantánamo Bay detention facility within a year; made public interrogation and torture memoranda from the Bush era; ordered a pay freeze on his cabinet; ordered compliance with the Freedom of Information Act; signed legislation against pay discrimination of women, known as the Lilly Ledbetter Act; extended health benefits to low-income children; and pushed through a $750-billion stimulus package with an emphasis on building up the domestic infrastructure through working with the states to create employment. Obama had hoped that his performance as an ideal exception would have garnered bipartisan support in the U.S. House of Representatives, but no Republican congressperson supported his stimulus bill. It was the Democratic Party's majority that enabled it to go to the Senate, where it was able to pass without a Republican filibuster.

This portrait of the early days of his administration suggests that although there may be a schism between the projections of idealization and idolization on President Obama and the man himself, the fact that Obama acted on some of what he promised to do reduces that gap. In a textbook response to our argument of subaltern speech against subalterns, the Republican Party responded first by choosing an African American, Michael Steele, to be its chief representative and, after Obama gave his February 2009 speech on the state of the economy, Governor Bobby Jindal of Louisiana, a dark-brown South Asian American, presented the Republican response. Their emergence in the Republican leadership as a response to Obama brought to the fore the underlying crassness of the Republican Party leadership's interpretation of the historical circumstance: The pressing social issues raised by the worldwide popularity of Obama at the dawn of his presidency were, for the Republican leadership, subsumed by the more mysterious project of securing, in Steele's and Jindal's racial and ethnic identities, his magic. There is, however, another set of considerations raised by another recent exemplification of the ideal exception—namely, Nelson Mandela, to whom we will now turn.

Our bringing up Nelson Mandela, the former president of South Africa, reveals that our observations on the postcolonial politics of race are not limited to the United States. Much of the grammar we have outlined from Booker T. Washington and Du Bois to King and Obama can be found in South Africa. There, the apartheid government was a textbook example of settler appeals to a founding premised upon *terra nullius*. By misrepresenting the Native population as outside of civilization and modernity, the South African state erected a system of ward and guardian preserved through ongoing violence. The anti-apartheid struggle produced a variety of brilliant spokespersons, many of whom functioned as voices of moral disapprobation of the system. Particularly striking, however, was the level of violence meted out against those whose efforts were more clearly *political*. Many were assassinated. Among them were Steve Bantu Biko and Martin Thembisile Hani, more widely known as Chris Hani. The former was the most influential theoretician of the Black Consciousness movement, and the latter was the leader of the South African Communist Party at the time of his assassination in 1993. The South African apartheid state was antiblack and anti-Communist.[73]

Biko, in particular, through a series of articles under the pseudonym Frank Talk—which, as with Kierkegaard's pseudonyms, were more pen names since the South African readers knew that he was the author of those articles—offered a conception of blackness as explicitly political. As a political identity, Black Consciousness brought together a multiracial coalition of East Indians, Coloreds (mixed people of Native African and Afrikaner or Dutch descent), and even some whites under a form of consciousness united against the South African racist state. War was in effect waged against the expression of Black Consciousness, which took the form of speech and organization—in a word, politics.[74] As the state became more repressive, the space available for speech in South African society shrank in sufficient measure to create an isomorphic relationship between speech and dissent. The antiblack state became the antipolitical one. A different tactic then emerged against the political as Black Consciousness, and that was the moral supervening over the political. The release of Nelson Mandela, the transformation of South Africa into a post-apartheid state through the construction of a new, antiracist constitution, the 1994 national elections that included all citizens, and the emergence of Nelson Mandela as the first president of that new government and the first Native African president of that country were effected with a moral power with global resonance.

For our analysis, what was crucial along the way was the transformation of Mandela, whose earlier efforts with the African National Congress led to his conviction of treason and his imprisonment on Robben Island. Through distancing himself from more radical black voices of protests, which included divorcing his wife Winnie Mandela avowedly because of her violent activities during the anti-apartheid struggle, and emerging as hope for white South Africans, Mandela's hybrid moral symbolism was marked by his sharing the Nobel Peace Prize in 1993 with Frederik Willem de Klerk (the last president of the apartheid-era South Africa). Mandela, as moral symbol, muted the voices that opposed that other dimension of the previous South African state, namely, its anti-Communism.[75] As Mandela declared on May Day in 1994: "In our economic policies ... there is not a single reference to things like nationalization, and this is not accidental. There is not a single slogan that will connect us with any Marxist ideology."[76] In his inaugural address, Obama, too, issued an attack on Communism, although in the American context a decade and a half later, only the most paranoid anti-Communists entertained the notion of such a threat to the United States. Thomas Frank recounts how "The apartheid government made an ideal love-match for the American far right. . . . It was also one of the only spots on planet Earth where the crackpot social theory of the far right—in which communists are everywhere and liberals are their 'useful idiots'— was the official ideology of the state. Indeed, white South Africa had staked its very existence on this lunacy. Claiming they faced a 'total onslaught' from secretive and superpowerful communist foes, the government had made it a crime not merely to *be* a Communist, but to *agree* with the Communist Party about certain things."[77] The American right-wing supporters of apartheid South Africa organized a strategy that took a path through apartheid-state-funded libertarian rewriting of apartheid as anti-capitalist so they could defend capitalism as a necessary feature of the post-apartheid state. "More amazing still," writes Frank,

is that the South African free marketers essentially got what they wanted, albeit more because of the IMF [International Monetary Fund] than the IFF [International Freedom Foundation, which was funded by the apartheid-era South African state]. The country's new constitution was indeed written to protect private property. The apartheid government began the privatizing, and the ANC [African National Congress], once it controlled the state, embarked on one of the most ambitious deregulatory schemes in the world. It sold off state-run operations from airports to waterworks. The results have been precisely what you'd expect: spectacular prosperity for some, little improvement for everyone else. In fact, and although it's difficult to believe, income inequality in South Africa has actually widened since apartheid was dismantled. South Africa is again a one-party state, with rampant corruption and Afrikaner-style cronyism. But money—thank God—is free at last.[78]

As neoliberalism became the ideology of the post–apartheid South African state that rapidly and radically deregulated state-run operations, as reparations and other considerations of justice went to the hands of whites, and as even public confessionals of Truth and Reconciliation were more unilateral (more blacks confessing, fewer whites doing so), the cries of opposition were muffled by the shared weight imposed by a moral symbolism that could not translate into anything less than ideal. South Africa became a beacon, a shining light of pride in antiracist struggle that covered continued, more rigorous racist practices, rationalized by the emergence of a small black elite while a large black majority sank into deeper squalor and despair.[79] The misery of the latter fell into a sign continuum of which divine warning became not only the fears of crime and xenophobic violence in South Africa but also the visual iconoclasm and voice of protest, treated as monstrous grunts and groans, of the shackdwellers' movement or the movement of the poors.[80] The shackdwellers and the poors now stand in relation to the new South African state as divine warnings facing the repression of that society's sign continua.[81]

The Mandela and the Obama phenomena, we are arguing, are connected to a development in postcolonies in the new millennium on the relationship of politics to civil society, namely, the moralistic war on the political discussed in chapter one—that is, a triumphant response to declared victory over the very possibility of threat of revolution by the downtrodden. The political spectrum marked here is one not of far left through far right but of right of center to far right. Associated with the left are the political and its links to governmental expectations that have faced erosion of public support when focused on populations of color, especially blacks, and when requiring centralized, government planning aimed at nurturing robust social democracy. The result is a transformation of the colonial condition of speechless monsters, where divine warnings are muted, to a postcolonial one of hybrid mediations by which colonial structures could be affirmed without the shame of being seen.

Monsters are now appearing to speak because there is an expansion of identification with monsters. In popular culture, they have become sexy and often objects of vicarious projection. One can, for instance, find many websites for vampire "meet-up" groups in which participants speak of recently having been "turned" and ready to feed their hunger. There is a connection between such identification and the varieties of "playing black," as well as playing *lumpenproletariat* (as in, for example, the Quentin Tarantino films), in an age of neoliberalism and neoconservatism—an age in which there has been an abrogation of responsibility for the infrastructure on which public well-being depends. Such identification is a form of bad faith akin to jumping into water in order to avoid being damp. Its effect, even if perceived only as the latest in adolescent rebellion, is to disarm the signifying function of monstrosity. By making an ever-increasing number of people, including the self, into monsters associated with unusual strength and desire, the warnings can be ignored, because as its exemplar, as a sign in the sign continuum, each manifestation points beyond itself, which amounts to ignoring the warning exemplified by monsters.

The point about monsters is that they should stimulate the search for what has gone wrong. Monsters, divine warnings, are supposed to make us question our society. It is no accident that increased monster identification is occurring in an age in which, as we argued earlier, many people are afraid of judgment. By shifting to equal-opportunity-monstrosity, no one can be responsible for the society because everyone has become its victim.

◇

5

Ruin

"Humanity is the greatest ruin," declares Robert Ginsberg. He continues: "Mythology and theology, philosophy's hand-mades, identify us as fallen. The Golden Age preceded our history. It is the happy state we left behind."[1] Ruin is a child of disaster. As fallen, as collapsed, humanity faces a tragic situation, echoed, according to Nietzsche, in Greek tragedy as a suffering avoidable only through having never been born, through never having come into being.

A disaster, a fall from the heavens and its inaugurated sign continuum, always occurs somewhere at some time. We have come to know such a convergence of space and time as a "disaster area." Such a place is in ruins. Somewhere, once teeming with life, once living in the ebb and flow of time, something at some time fell to the wayside, commencing a process of decay, perhaps from destruction, leading to the petrifying of past hopes. The Earth is littered with remains, historical in some cases, passing the eyes of most of us in others, many of which revealed a good fight against nature, as when a wobble of the planet turned lush fields into deserts and forced ancient civilizations to endure for as long as they could, which they had hoped would be forever. At some point, there were the final steps as the last dwellers moved on. One emigrates to live, but as Jean-Paul Sartre had reflected on exhaustion, the point at which one abandons a project is not always an externally imposed necessity.[2] "I cannot go on," is often said when one could take at least another step. There is a point at which inhabitants abandon the project of the place, the point at which "here" becomes the place at which one can no longer live, the place at which the expectations for the self can no longer be realized.

In other instances, the moment is cataclysmic. Death and destruction, as suffered by a village or city on a volcanic site, are instantaneous. In others, agents of destruction come in the form of human reapers, razing communities to the ground, decimating their infrastructure, with the rapidity of furies from the heavens. And then, there are plagues, infestations, and disease eating away at life, spreading through the halls, infecting even the sociality of human life through the poisoning of proximity, rendering deadly the pleasure of touch and the warmth of breath. Such disasters at first leave a haunted presence of life in the wake of the flight taken by the uninfected, but in time, as abandoned homes, neglected streets, whole infrastructures are left to the ravages of bacteria, dust, and wind, the ruined remains no longer stand as a site of sudden flight but an above-ground necropolis, indistinguishable from many other dead places.

We have been arguing against the naturalization of disaster or the spirit of seriousness, the materializing of values imposed upon the world, toward disaster. A similar criticism pertains to ruins. A ruin is a peculiarly human phenomenon. It is the remains of a human project that has ceased. The distinction is evident in the comparison, for instance, of the town and bay of Porto in Corsica, and the remains of the ancient Roman city of Pompeii in Italy. The former is a majestic seaside World Heritage Site wonder available to the world. Its beautiful red rock formations are the results of a volcanic eruption. Pompeii, today an important archaeological site also formed by a volcano, is a ruin. What remains is a day in which a vibrant city became a necropolis.

Ginsberg defines a ruin as "the irreparable remains of a human construction that, by a destructive act or process, no longer dwells in the unity of the original, but may have its own unities that we can enjoy."[3] In ruins, time has come to a halt. "Pompeii," Ginsberg observes, "has ruined time. Its walls are timeless wells. We dip into their absoluteness of being, beyond categories of time and purpose. The innate brickness of the bricks has all the time in the world to educate our sensibility to it. Roman civilization recedes in consciousness, as we give ourselves over fully to this civilization of bricks."[4] What Ginsberg is getting at transcends the facts of the materials strewn about at a disaster area and left in ruin. He is pointing to, in his reference to "civilization," the living community that once animated them with meaning. Recall Fanon's observation that society requires human beings for its continuation; it is a paradoxical structure that creates that by which it is created. Society, then, is an expression of human beings in the peculiar recognition of the same dynamic of being born from another while being responsible for itself and producing others. This dimension of human existence shared by its macro, societal correlate is its fundamental incompleteness. As with a human life, where there is birth, maturation, decline, death, there is a cyclical dynamic in societies, where, in the fervor of youth, they are lived as though they will do so forever. As the death of loved ones reminds each of us of our own mortality, so, too, do ruins edify societal hubris. The Twin Towers once stood above us and reached to the sky, exemplifying the force of a political economic ideology that has been announced as the end of history, only to have been crumbled into dust in a mixture of suffering and death at the hands of human agents and left as a disaster area in which attempted monuments cannot erase the signifier of ruin.

Whether the Roman Coliseum, the Parthenon, Inca Pyramids, or Thebes, these remains remind us of civilizations that once expected to last forever. They are testaments to the inevitable decay of all empires, cities, towns, villages, homes—none of these live forever because no one lives forever, and even where such expectations are hoped for through memory, even the latter depends on the longevity of others. We are not, in ourselves, the children by whom we are remembered. At some point, there will be none.

Existentialists echoing Jean-Jacques Rousseau, such as Sartre and Camus, have written of the human being as a figure condemned to freedom. Although this freedom is a manifestation of our responsibility for how we live, it is also an understanding of our incompleteness. Each human being faces her or his self and correlative communities as a bastion of possibilities, but in each lived moment, many possibilities are dried up, and the range of potential shrinks to the point of reflection on a narrative, if one is afforded such a luxury, on what could have been and what might still be possible. The message in life, Ginsberg argues, echoing Arthur Schopenhauer, is not happiness but to make ourselves ready when it is our time to die. In "The Road to Salvation," chapter forty-nine, in the second volume of *The World as Will and Representation*, Schopenhauer writes:

> There is only one inborn error [in humankind], and that is the notion that we exist in order to be happy ... We are nothing more than the will-to-live, and the successive satisfaction of all our willing is what we think of through the concept of happiness. So long as we

persist in this inborn error, ... the world seems to us full of contradictions.... We may still try to put the blame for our individual unhappiness now on the circumstances, now on other people, now on our own bad luck or even lack of skill, and we may know quite well how all these have worked together to bring it about, but this in no way alters the result, that we have missed the real purpose of life, which in fact consists in being happy. The consideration of this then often proves to be very depressing, especially when life is already drawing to an end; hence the countenances of almost all elderly persons wear the expression of what is called *disappointment*.... Pains and sorrows, ... prove very real, and often exceed all expectations. Thus everything in life is certainly calculated to bring us back from that original error, and to convince us that the purpose of our existence is not to be happy.[5]

Schopenhauer draws the argument to its conclusion in a meditation on death:

Dying is certainly to be regarded as the real aim of life; at the moment of dying, everything is decided which through the whole course of life was only prepared and introduced. Death is the result, the *résumé*, of life, or the total sum expression at one stroke [of] all the instruction given by life in detail and piecemeal, namely that the whole striving, the phenomenon of which is life, was a vain, fruitless, and self-contradictory effort, to have returned from which is a deliverance. Just as the whole slow vegetation of the plant is related to the fruit that at one stroke achieves a hundredfold what the plant achieved gradually and piecemeal, so is life with its obstacles, deluded hopes, frustrated plans, and constant suffering related to death, which at one stroke destroys all, all that the persons has willed and thus crowns the instruction given him by life.[6]

In addition to Nietzsche, who was also inspired by Schopenhauer, Ginsberg probably had passages like the one just quoted in mind when he declares that "To philosophize is to ruin the human being."[7] Yet he agrees with Schopenhauer: "We are the species living under the death sentence (Swed.: *dömda*, 'judged,' 'punished,' 'condemned,' 'doomed') that it has passed against itself."[8] And he adds the existential situation of humanity in the new millennium: "The one constant truth for all humanity has been that we are each going to die. What differentiates the present generation from our predecessors is that we also bear the cross of destroying the species. If such a thing as sin exists, this is it. Killing a god might be forgiven by humanity, but we cannot forgive killing humanity."[9]

Although we are all condemned to death, it makes all the difference to each of us whether that shared fate is something any of us, in our life story, deserves. This is a problem shared by the individual and society. Karl Jaspers has written of this problem as *Die Schuldfrage*, the guilt/blame/responsibility question.[10] The term *Schuld* is related to the German word *Schule* (school), which reveals the educational dimension of the concept. The notion of guilt without learning is pointless and, in many instances, pathological. Jaspers was thinking through the disaster wrought by the actions of the German government, many of the German people, and their allies, and the general responsibility shared by German citizens leading up to, during, and after World War II. He outlined four kinds of guilt with correlated responsibilities: metaphysical, ethical and moral, legal, and political. The first pertains to one's relationship with G-d or existence throughout the universe; the second is a relationship with the rules and mores of one's society and one's relationship with one's self; the third is a matter of positive law; and the last is the responsibility every member of a society has for the actions of its government. The last, as he addressed it to his fellow Germans at the end of World War II, raises the question of whether a people's government has acted in a manner that affords a good case for mercy in the instance of its defeat. Jaspers asks every government to remember that it is the people, its citizens, who will suffer the debt, and in some instances the death sentence, of such a trial. Returning to Schopenhauer and Ginsberg, if life is about preparing for not deserving to die, would it not be a disaster for a government or a society to have failed to offer the same for its people? Ginsberg admits:

> We are responsible for our extermination. Efforts exist to attribute the blame to the culprits among us: the rulers, greedy, hostile, thoughtless, doctrinaire, military, otherworldly, Other. But they are our fellows. The blame is upon us for failing to control them or guide them to the light. Looking for an escapegoat, we also cast blame on the System, economic order, communication gap, uneven distribution of resources, violence of television, limitations of education, inhibitions of tradition, intolerance of religion. Yet, at heart, we know that human beings are victims of ourselves, not of circumstances. We allow circumstances and systems to get in our way.... The destruction of the world falls upon our head, if we fail to stop it.... You and I are obligated to save the world.... To be human requires action to save the world. Such action is without expectation of success. It need not be accompanied by hope.[11]

We have arrived at a new development in the continuum of disastrous signification. Such reflection occasions apocalyptic imagery ancient and new, as Jean Comaroff and John Comaroff have argued in their work on millennial capitalism.[12] We are speaking, of course, of the end of the world. From the perspective of empires, which reached across national boundaries in the hope to stretch across space and time into eternity, their destruction is no less than that. And although the remains of past empires mock such efforts, contemporary empires and world powers ignore them and continue to stretch forth with an abiding sense of necessity.

The world can, however, end not in a great cataclysm but through a quiet and perhaps unnoticed whimper. When we wrote of colonialism in the previous chapter, we also referred to the epistemic practices, the signs and symbols through which meaning is made manifest in the social world, in a word, *culture*. What can a society do when the sign continuum of the end of the world is the death of its culture?

In the summer of 2008, the authors visited two "departments" of France: Guadeloupe and Corsica. An immediate distinction between them and similar island-nations under the protectorate of a First World power is that the French invested in their infrastructure, in contrast to what may be found in Puerto Rico or what was left of those in much of the Anglo-Caribbean. Having apparently learned their lessons from what happened in Vietnam and Algeria, France has organized the material conditions for a constant flow of French citizens from its periphery to its center in a very modern expectation of a universal Frenchness, in which a highly educated, French citizenry, even from island nations such as Guadeloupe and Corsica, speak of being the latter in the face of declining cultural specificity. Ghjuvanteramu Rocchi, Corsica's leading living poet and one of the creators of its written language, explores the meaning of being Corsican in a world where fewer Corsicans speak the language and most, going on generations, live outside their ancestral home. Once an island of 1,000,000 inhabitants, Corsica is now home to only 250,000. Each year, as Corsica becomes more of a tourist site, living Corsican culture seems to be disappearing.

We are reminded here of Jean-Jacques Rousseau's reflections on the challenges posed by the island of Corsica when he was asked to serve as its legislator, as the one who could enable its still emergent general will fully to flourish. Christopher Kelly writes that what interested Rousseau in this task was precisely the fact that the island was considered a European backwater, the opposite of French and English models of modern strong states. Kelly writes, "Rather than seeing Corsica as merely the uncivilized abode of bandits in need of colonial rule by a continental power, he regarded it as the one place in Europe still capable of receiving a sound legislation."[13] The framing question of Rousseau's work was how the island, formerly colonized by the Moors and then the Genoans, could aim to reach a genuinely postcolonial state: how to move it out of conditions of economic dependence and poverty. He surmised that that would require figuring out how to transform its primarily agricultural economy into an asset, most ambitiously how to translate its produce into international capital.

Rousseau insisted as Fanon would later that the aim was not to emulate former colonizers but to lead a concerted national effort to identify and cultivate its indigenous resources, most centrally *its people*. This would require Corsicans treating Corsica as its own economic and political center, rather than as an outpost or appendage to the political economy of the mother country of its colonizers. One indispensable resource for this project was that Corsicans were not decadent; they did not display the individual and collective vices of their supposedly more civilized Western counterparts. This, for Rousseau, meant that they remained spirited. Still, this strength could easily collapse into widespread banditry, especially if people grew impatient with the project of building a legitimate democratically governed state. Rousseau argued that they did not need to become different from how they were but to preserve this in the absence of a shared enemy that united them across differences. They could do this by directing these forces toward maintaining their independence.

Rousseau insisted that the characterization of Corsica as a *lumpenproletarian* island of people more inclined to be thieves than hard-working citizens obscured the origins of these predilections in the culture of colonialism itself. He wrote,

> Who would not be seized with horror against a barbarous Government that, in order to see these unfortunate people cutting each other's throats, did not spare any effort for inciting them to do so? Murder was not punished; what am I saying, it was rewarded ... [I]t had as its goal making more onerous these same taxes which it did not dare to increase, always holding the Corsicans in abasement by attaching them so to speak to their soil, by turning them away from commerce, the arts, from all the lucrative professions, by keeping them from rising up, from being educated, from becoming rich. Its

goal was to get all produce dirt cheap from the monopolies of its officials. It took every measure for draining the Island of money in order to make it necessary there, and in order always to keep it from returning to it. Tyranny could not apply a more refined maneuver, while appearing to favor cultivation, it succeeded in crushing the nation; it wanted to reduce it to a heap of base peasants living in the most deplorable misery.[14]

In other words, Corsicans had come to deplore labor not only because it was a pure loss to them but also because it was a seemingly permanent and destructive sentence. It was from this condition that Rousseau hoped the Corsicans could mature. He recommended a temporary isolationism that would enable the island to increase the interdependence of its regions and their people, making a culture of cultivating and depending on their own forces.[15] Unlike town dwellers, rural people both had more children and were more attached to their soil, satisfied by a simple and rustic life that inspired no longing for change. Unlike commerce that produced wealth and dependence and rebelliousness and softness, agriculture could assure the predispositions necessary to freedom.

Rousseau underscored the appropriateness of different governmental forms to different environments and argued that such a rustic place was best fit for a democracy. Ironically, the counties and jurisdictions that the colonists had introduced and the destruction of the local nobility that they had overseen would facilitate a transformation in this direction. He insisted that political creativity would be necessary to make the different parts of the island economically interdependent so that the administrative capital would not thrive as everywhere else fell into economic stagnation. This meant avoiding creating a small group of cities that drew aspiring bourgeoisies that produced nothing. A government surely did require a center, but this would be a purely administrative one that public men occupied only temporarily before returning to the other dimensions of their lives. Rousseau hoped this might forestall the drawing of cultivators away from the countryside that would be and would have to be affirmed as Corsica's real source of strength.[16]

Rousseau sought to figure out how to link political privileges not to amassed wealth but to productive labor. He therefore sought to avoid what he considered the debasing introduction of money, arguing instead for the use of a strict system of exchange. He explained that money was useful only as a sign of inequality, particularly for foreigners. One could make exchanges of goods themselves without mediating values, creating storehouses in certain essential places. Ultimately, he reminded his readers that political independence, their ultimate aim, requires that all lived well without becoming rich. Thus he encouraged the emerging government to award political privileges based on which citizens produced most. He insisted repeatedly that the ease and health of politics were two fundamentally different concerns and that the latter should be their focus. In the absence of money and taxation, citizens could be asked to contribute in kind, through labor. If roads needed to be built, it would be the citizenry who would have to do it.

Rousseau concluded with reflections about the qualities of human beings. Here echoing Thomas Hobbes's *Leviathan*, he wrote that it is fear and hope that govern men.[17] Parting company there he qualified that fear only holds people back lest they not face punishment, that it is only hope that can lead men and women to act. The task then was to awaken the nation's activity, literally to give it ground for great hopes. Not a hope linked to sensual pleasure, but to a substantive pride that he explained involves "esteeming oneself based on truly estimable goods."[18] Nothing, he wrote, is more "really beautiful than independence and power." What could sustain this character of a newly articulated nation was to maintain and deepen activity and life in the entire state by paying close attention to the emerging nature of civil power, to assure that it would take the form of legitimate authority rather than abusive wealth. With the latter, Rousseau noted, where wealth dominated, power and authority would be separate—to obtain wealth and authority were two separate tasks with the implication that apparent power was with elected officials while real power was with the rich who could buy their authority. Such practices could only lead to disappointment that would spread languor through the Island. The greatest asset of the Corsicans was their rustic way of life and their spiritedness. They were capable of freedom rather than merely obedience. But the cultivation of a viable political economy was an indispensable basis for and would signal the emergence of legitimate governance and of the general will.

In Guadeloupe, the markers of race ironically enable the majority Afro-Caribbean population to forge a Caribbean identity through which French inclusion is not tantamount to disappearance: It is not only the beguine that is preserved in Guadeloupe but a continued, although often ambivalent, negotiation with the Creole language. But even for Guadeloupeans, the question of whether the ultimate relationship of French to Creole is such that the future will one day hold the absorption of the latter into the former haunts every cultural act. Reflecting on the Africana Francophone world of which Guadeloupe is a part, Wandia Njoya observes, "As far as the [French] Republic is concerned, Africans have no history, culture or identity other than that which the Republic approves. Africans who adhere to its ideals are therefore compelled to see themselves and the world through its eyes. They also ignore, diminish or deny the history of France that does not conform to these ideals, in the vain hope that the Republic will respond by treating them with the respect and dignity accorded to French citizens."[19]

This problem of looming cultural extinction is not, however, new, as similar questions marked similar struggles in antiquity. Greece and then Rome, after all, offered for ancient Jews the challenge of modernization, the result of which has been the emergence of Rabbinic Judaism, the complex intellectual and spiritual struggle of reconciling the Hellenic, Roman, and Hebrew worlds, and a debate on the cultural location of Judaism to this day.[20] Similar concerns abound on the place of the Arabic world in North Africa, the varieties of mainland Northeast Asian civilizations on the Pacific Islands, including the indigenous peoples of what is today Japan. And in the Americas, this problem of cultural disaster unfolded in the genocidal practices that reduced the numbers of Native populations and then through the cultural hegemony of Spain and Portugal in the south and England and France in the north. There are still speakers of these languages, but many fear, in concert with Ghjuvanteramu Rocchi, the impending cultural equivalence of the end of the world.

For some, cultural disaster takes the form of a ruined existence. There are, all over the world, people living through cultural ruin or culture on the verge of ruin. The struggle of continuation is Promethean. For some, the struggle for cultural continuity drags cultural practice out of the stream of mundane life to the level of sacrifice and fanatic devotion. Religious fundamentalisms are the perverse bedfellows of cultural preservation. How could certain cultural practices become relevant across all time without war on the future? If subsequent generations must be bound to past ones in an eternal circle of the same, would not the effect become one of never truly having been born? There are many myths about parents refusing the birth of the next generation: Among the ancient Greeks, Ouranos (sky) refused to let his children emerge from the birth canal of their mother Gaia (earth). Kronos, one of the sons, took the option of castrating his father and throwing his genitalia into the sea from which sprang Aphrodite. Among the Hebrews, disobedience in the form of eating from the fruit of knowledge leads to expulsion from paradise, and an endless chain of sacrifices, of humanity to G-d, of children to elders, offer a narrative of election as the responsibility to offer, preserve, and protect G-d's words on earth. There, prayers as sacrifice remind younger generations that theirs is to give, the giving, the *Mitzvot*. The G-d that gives also demands, and demands much. What happens to Judaism, many Jews worry, when generations emerge who wish no longer to give but only to take?[21]

All over the world, the youth are losing their youthfulness. The burden of living one's life is already unbearable. To add the weight of one's people and one's culture, as has been the lot of colonized peoples, beckons the dreaded tide of lost horizons. Exhaustion lurks.

Cultural disaster leads to a rallying of forces against the future. It demands sacrifice of the young. Richard Fenn, in *The Secularization of Sin*, reads modern burdens on the youth through ancient grammars of sacrifice devoid of their original telos or purpose.[22] Using the Daedalus myth as inspiration, Fenn argues against institutions of authority that deploy mystifying practices to hold sway over the youth and possibilities of growth into responsible adulthood. Recall that Daedalus was the gifted technician who built the labyrinth to hide away the Minotaur, the offspring of Pasiphaë's (King Minos's queen) lusty union with the white bull given to Minos by Poseidon for sacrifice to the gods. Fenn reads the myth as a tale of insatiable greed with consequences so ugly that additional precautions of subterfuge were needed. Minos's greed led to his keeping the bull instead of giving it to the gods; Pasiphaë's greed led to her masquerading as a cow to satisfy her lust for the bull; and the offspring, the Minotaur, lurks in the labyrinth where he consumes the youth lost in the maze. Minos's untrustworthiness and greed continued in his imprisoning Daedalus and his son Icarus, no doubt with the hope of having permanent access to Daedalus' technical genius, in a tower overlooking the sea. Daedalus then orchestrated their escape by devising wings with which they flew over the open waters. He had warned Icarus not to fly too high, however, since the wings were secured with wax and would melt, and not too low since he could be swept up by the sea. Mesmerized by the experience of flight, Icarus attempted to fly to the sun, whereupon the heat melted the wax, and he plummeted to his death in the waters below. The myth, Fenn contends, offers a tale of sacrifice, purification, and the pressures of older generations on the young: Icarus is admonished by his father not to fly too high or too low but to follow him, as many exemplars of patriarchal authority, the Daedalus Complex, do. Icarus's fall reveals two poles of purification, namely, fire and water, which, we should add, exemplify masculine and feminine considerations in ancient Greek mythology. Burnt by the masculine force (the sun), Icarus fell to the feminine one (water, the womb), the source of all life. Thus, there is the greed manifested in institutions of power, the king and the queen, which consumes the people, and then there is the sacrifice by which purification is sought for the debt of consumption.

In the modern world, where the mythic foundations of rituals of purification have been lost, a legitimation crisis emerges for institutions that demand sacrifices of the people, especially across generations. "When the Minotaur is clearly the government or banking system, there is no abiding reason for either tribute or sacrifice. The Protestant miracle is that so many are still willing to make their sacrifices to the larger society."[23] Writing at the end of the Reagan era of unbridled greed, Fenn's ruminations portended the pyramid scheme behavior in the financial and real estate markets that led to the situation of world financial ruin by the end of the George W. Bush administration and the dawn of Barack Obama's. The sacrifices are many, and who else will inherit the large debts for the bailout of the banking industry and other aspects of economies not only in the United States, but also many worldwide, but everyone else, especially subsequent generations? Amazingly, the reluctance to bail out the automobile industry in the U.S. could be compared to hesitance to lend $14 to someone after lending $700, given the sums of $700 billion for the finance banks in the face of the automobile industry's request for $14 billion.[24] For our purposes, the divine warning represented by economic monsters, which in the age of neoliberalism is socialism, is the dimension of the self, of the avowed better system, pushed from sight in a maze of confusion similar to the financial instruments used to bamboozle much of the public worldwide, although not entirely so since greed enabled institutions ranging from university and hospital endowments to municipalities to look the other way while investing in things even their experts did not fully understand. As things fall apart, further distance is placed from the self through claims of adulteration: Somehow, the system has been polluted, and purification is called for.

Overlooked in the search for culprits, Fenn observes, is the demise of the individual as person versus institutional actors. What many of those who selfishly took from the system and its correlative institutions knew was that the latter would sacrifice them at the slightest sign of threat. They, as expendable, followed the paths against being swallowed up. "This leaves the individual as *person* a mere survivor of the labyrinth."[25] Purification demands rooting out purveyors of the pollution that has spread throughout the community, which in this case extends across the globe, and the expected rituals of cleansing, which in the past involved fire (burnings, electric chairs), water (drownings or rebirth through baptisms), or burial and resurrection (prison time). The accused continue to be the usual suspects: immigrants, social pariahs, and other members of the damned. But those are ultimately not enough to erase the burden placed on others rendered distant in the obfuscation of international hysteria, namely, the young and subsequent descendants. "Any community that seeks to restore primordial unities, to pay the debt of the individual to those who have gone before and to the world itself," writes Fenn, "is inevitably going to stimulate demands for an unbroken harmony with both the natural and social orders. That harmony will always be threatened by the young and the old, by aliens and intruders, and by those who represent impurities in the ideological or social system."[26] Those, however, whose domain is the future are of special interest: "Certainly the young, who like Icarus 'impede their fathers at their work' and seem to play when the serious rites of the community are at stake, can be scapegoated as a source not only of innovation but of threat to the community as a whole."[27]

In Fenn's analysis, we see the yoking of the young, discussed in the struggle against cultural disaster, brought to the understanding of debt in even the dominating society. The next generation is, in effect, forced to be the parents of those from whom they have descended by virtue of the debts they bear. Beyond the constraints of economic burdens are the cultural presuppositions lived in each generation as though permanent. Implicit in such presumption is the same cultural fear pushed to subterranean levels: that in whose demise is no less than the end of the world. The message from dying cultures, suffered in relations of the old to the young, is that all cultures ultimately die, and their signals, as divine warnings, are what all must learn—that in spite of avowed preservation for the sake of children and subsequent generations, the disaster of contemporary society, its sign continuum, is that by not facing our responsibilities we are ruining the future *as future* and are thereby making the case for a deserved vanquishing of humankind. It is stupid for humankind to expect to live forever. Schopenhauer, Ginsberg, and Fenn remind us, however, that life as a preparation for death involves taking seriously what one must do for the value of life. A society that fails to do such wastes what little time it has at the expense of others. Ignoring the signs is perilous. The testament to the unheeded divine warning of our age may be an epitaph of admonition from desperate final efforts. The youth, exhausted, eventually offer nothing but the end of the world.

◇

6

Dawn

Disasters, we have been arguing, are sign continua of things not immediately apparent. They, as with monsters, their correlates, are symptoms of more subterranean forces. Failure to read these signs often leads to efforts to erase them and, in doing so, avoid what they signify. Not having actually addressed the problems, the consequences often become direr than they need to be. Such problems never go away but fester. A humanity that refuses to answer encomia to mature is destined to destroy itself in a game of children playing with deadly weapons. In maturation is the messiness of life, of treating mistakes as opportunities from which to learn instead of dreaded signs of imperfection. Efforts at purification foreclose the future by presuming the return of sanctified origins.

The creature in Mary Shelley's *Frankenstein* chooses to incinerate himself. Impure, unnatural pollution, scientific and metaphysical, he burns himself in the frozen north, a cold womb, a metaphor of returning to death, from which he was born. Fire is his chosen method of purification. In vampire lore, such creatures, pollution as they are, die from the morning sun's purifying rays, and they could also be harmed by holy water. In Christian representations of the underworld, sinners are tormented by fire, which could be read as a long sentence of eternal purification. The sun and the sea, as two directions of purification, encompass Icarus's fate of reaching to one but falling into the other. In sunrise, there is not only purification but also hope, and in the sea, there is the vast expanse of possibility. Our attachments could become such that we never find Ariadne's thread and our way out of the labyrinth. As we have argued, the maze from which we seek freedom is of our own design. A social world weighted down by the sediment of

117

evaded responsibilities, spirits of seriousness, and closed epistemic structures accepts few opportunities to see itself. Given global warming, will global conflagration, biblical methods of purifying cities of iniquity, be our lot?

Dante of Alighieri offered some insight on our misguided attachments in his epic Christian portrait of the place of purifying evil in his *Inferno*. At the heart of "Hell" is the classic direction of consumed hatred. After guiding Dante's protagonist, elicited in the first-person, through a tormenting, concentric labyrinth of poetic justice, which included the Minotaur in the seventh encircled level, Virgil brings him to the icy depths of the ninth one, where traitors are trapped close to Satan himself. The traitors are frozen from the neck down, and two of them, Count Ugolino and Archbishop Ruggieri, catch Dante's attention. Ugolino, chewing on the head of Ruggieri, pauses only to tell the tale of the wrongs done to him by the latter. At the center is Satan, frozen from the waist down, chewing on the greatest traitors of history, including Judas, betrayer of Christ. The images are a revelation of consuming hatred, which enslaves the unforgiving. At this point, Virgil guides Dante outside, to the night's sky at the coming dawn, where he is able "to see—once more—the stars."[1]

Dante's poem, although filled with themes of purification, brings to the fore, in his own understanding, the dimensions of the self and societal vices often denied or disavowed. That it is he being guided through, on a divine mission, raises the question of what is to be learned from such admonitions. The core message of things of which to let go, of how such attachments destroy even the future, is instructive of what creates hell on earth. The allegory of looking to the stars before dawn, to the heavens, is the counterpoint of disaster. Although a fall from the heavens is a form of ruin, what is gained by looking onto those signs before sunrise is a reminder of things heavenly and a new day.

The grammar of Dante's poem resonates in modern thoughts of liberation. Although Marx and Engels advised the proletariat to beware of opiates of the people, they also advanced the view that ideology maintains slavery through obfuscation and mystification. The guiding force of dialectical science promised the breaking of chains and the ushering in of a social world of greater freedom and humanity. Their predecessor, G. W. F. Hegel, offered a similar story of the dialectical unfolding of freedom, although, as his *Philosophy of Right* attested, he had faith in the market and modern secular state for the conditions of ethical life. Fanon, however, saw less inevitability to the processes of emancipation. Agreeing with the spirit of the dialectical unfolding of freedom, he added the realization that oftentimes those who initiate the process of liberation become the greatest impediments to its subsequent development. This insight, which we call the Moses Syndrome, comes to this: those who could lead us to the Promised Land are not necessarily the best equipped to govern us there. It may be best that they do not enter. Fanon regarded the task as one of facing the trauma involved in getting so far and realizing what must be transcended in order to go farther. This is what Fanon ultimately means when, echoing *L'internationale*, he implores us all to acquire a *"peau neuve, développer une pensée neuve, tenter de mettre sur pied un homme neuf."*[2] In our translation: to acquire "new skin, develop new thought, and set afoot a new man [humanity]."

While the eighteenth century and much of the twentieth-century could be considered an age of revolution, the last years of the twentieth have inaugurated a period of anti-revolution marked by the ascendance of global neoliberalism with the political spectrum being such that even left liberal countries of Western Europe were being pulled to the right by pressures from neoconservative regimes. The reality is that the conditions upon which revolutionary demands were premised still remain. Enslavement of much of humankind has increased, hunger in a world of plenty has grown, and environmental conditions for the end of us all are exacerbated by governmental policies and socioeconomic expectations that amount to putting our heads in the sand. The future seems to be of little concern in our age because the young, although valorized, are ultimately envied perhaps to the point of hatred. Their future seems to lack the requisite conditions to become "ours." That future, as "theirs," seems to have become irrelevant in an age of greed, which, in its logical consequence, cannot even see what is "ours" but only what is "mine."

In Hannah Arendt's essay, "Crisis in Education," she argues that all living things, whether they are plants, polities, or people, need, in addition to light, the security of darkness, or some refuge from the brightness of the public world, to grow. Public places are those in which we reveal who, in addition to what, we are. To put children into such a spotlight too early is a form of abandonment and betrayal. The eradication of a coherent distinction between public and private worlds obscures the indispensable need of children for places of relative concealment in order to mature. What schools should do, Arendt argues, is to mediate between private and public life, creating a transitional sphere in which children and young adults can practice being a human being beneath the radar of an unforgiving and unforgetting public record. The school, she explained, represents the world, but is not identical with it. This is its unique value.[3]

For schools actually to offer such a space, educators must be assured in their role as representatives of the world as it is. They will not have made it what it is and may wish that it was otherwise, but they must be able to say authoritatively, "This is our world" and it is toward it that our education leads. It is a disaster, in Arendt's view, to encourage young students to throw off educational authorities and adults as one might urge the proletariat or colonized people to do with the bourgeoisie or their colonizers. Marxist and anticolonial models are political ones and, as such, pertain to the failures of adults to emerge as equals within shared polities. Education, by contrast, involves temporarily protecting the world from its children and children from the world. This quarantine is required to cultivate young people as a new generation that can emerge in its own right. To prepare its members with slogans about what is wrong rather than focusing neutrally on the development of their minds is actually, Arendt claims, to interrupt their chance to come into the world with their own moment to try to set it right. One must, in other words, studiously avoid prematurely thrusting children into adult battles that would stunt their own ability to grow into the very adults that could wage such struggles in their own right. It is not that one must strive to be apolitical, but that one must not encourage premature pessimism and cynicism that may primarily be a reflection of one's own feelings of political impotence.

We have criticized the project of turning away from monsters and have argued for learning from them, reading the signs they signify. If our analysis is correct, then, as we gaze upon that which has fallen, which means to look upon ourselves, instead of shuddering with dread and running away, we should see our present circumstance as an opportunity to make good of what is to come. We, each generation of humanity, have been asked to save the world. We are fortunate that there may still be enough time.

◇

Notes

Note for Beginning

1. There is much debate over the number of people killed, injured, and displaced. *The Guardian* in the UK on November 30, 2006, reported that 300,000 people died on December 26, 2004, when the wave hit. In 2005, *BBC News* reported that 130,000 had died in Indonesia, 31,000 in Sri Lanka, 8,850 in Southeast India, 1,900 on the Andaman and Nicobar Islands, 5,395 in Thailand, 81 in Maldives, 68 in Malaysia, two in Bangladesh, between 150 and 200 in Somalia, 1 person in Kenya, 10 in Tanzania, and 1 in the Seychelles; the military junta reported 61 in Myanmar, but the World Food Program estimated a number closer to or more than 200. This tally suggests a number closer to 178,000 confirmed deaths. *The New Zealand Herald*, on which we have drawn, in 2007 reported 230,000 dead or missing.

Notes for Chapter 1

1. Richard Cavendish, *A History of Magic* (London, UK: Arkana, 1987), p. 36. In Charity Cannon Willard's biography of Christine de Pizan, she explains that at the University of Bologna in the fourteenth century, then the center of medical studies in Europe, the course leading to the degree of doctor included the study of astrology "as the constellations were thought to govern not only the destiny of the individual but also the various members of one's body at specified seasons of the year" and practice in the art of rhetoric in the hope that physicians would be able to persuade their patients to "submit to the treatments ... prescribed." See Charity Cannon Willard, *Christine de Pizan: Her Life and Works* (New York: Persea, 1984), p. 17.

2. It is striking, as well, that catastrophe has the word *astro* wedged within it, so as to demarcate the ill fate of a fallen star or planet. Things that fall from the heavens embody a form of suffering that cannot fully be understood by those who see them, only, from below.

3. Cavendish, *A History of Magic*, p. 36.

4. *Ibid*, p. 37.

5. See our discussion of damnation, below.

6. We will develop our discussion of monsters in the next chapter.

7. Little media attention is paid to survivors of 9/11, individuals who were in the trade towers and who managed to escape. We hear, in documentaries and news coverage commemorating the event, much more from the loved ones of those who did not make it. See our concluding remarks on survivors at the end of this chapter. For discussion, see, e.g., Christine M. Roedigue, "Media Coverage of the Events of 9/11" (2002), http://www.csulb.edu/~rodrigue/bldr911.html. Cf. also, Shankar Vedantam, "Along with Grief, 9/11 Survivors Find Resolve," *The Washington Post* (September 10, 2007); and Dennis Sadowski, "Meeting Pope at Ground Zero Brings Tears to Sept. 11 Survivor," *The Catholic News Service* (April 29, 2008), http://www.catholicnews.com/data/stories/cns/0802366.htm.

8. Albert Camus, *The Stranger*, trans. Stuart Gilbert (New York: Vintage, 1954).

9. There have been many forums and publications devoted to spelling out this event. For a concise and rich portrait of the demonization of the victims of that catastrophe, see Henry A. Giroux, *Stormy Weather: Katrina and the Politics of Disposability* (Boulder, CO: Paradigm Publishers, 2006).

10. Timothy Chambers, "'They're Finding Food, but We're Looting?': A Two-Ethics Model for Racist Double Standards," *APA Newsletter on Philosophy and the Black Experience* 6, no. 1 (Fall 2006): 5–7.

11. See, e.g., Chambers, *ibid*,; and Giroux, *Stormy Weather*, pp. 48–53.

12. Michel Foucault, *Discipline and Punish: Birth of the Prison*, trans. Alan Sheridan (New York: Vintage, 1977), pp. 198–199. Foucault observes that the leper, who was the symbolic inhabitant of the space of exclusion, is incorporated into the model of the plague victim. The technique of excluding him also makes use of disciplinary partitioning and individualization to mark and brand the normal and abnormal.

13. Although our approach is phenomenological in orientation, we find affinity with this notion in Bourdieu's thought, which, in spite of his criticisms of phenomenology, is not incompatible with similar reflections in the thought of Maurice Merleau-Ponty and Frantz Fanon, especially the latter's concerns with sociogenesis in the colonial and racial context. To offer a developed discussion of this point will take us too far away from our subject. Bourdieu's meaning of "field" is offered in a variety of his works. See, e.g., Pierre Bourdieu, *The Logic of Practice*, trans. Richard Nice (Stanford, CA: Stanford University Press, 1980), *Pascalian Meditations*, trans. Richard Nice (Stanford, CA: Stanford University Press, 1997), and for exegesis of the concept, Terry Rey, *Bourdieu on Religion: Imposing Faith and Legitimacy* (London: Equinox Publishing LTD, 2007), pp. 44–46. Fanon raises sociogenesis in *Black Skin, White Masks*, trans.

Charles Lamm Markman (New York: Grove, 1967). For discussion, see Lewis R. Gordon, "Is the Human a Teleological Suspension of Man?: A Phenomenological Exploration of Sylvia Wynter's Fanonian and Biodicean Reflections," in *After Man, Towards the Human: Critical Essays on the Thought of Sylvia Wynter*, ed. by Anthony Bogues (Kingston, JA: Ian Randle, 2006), pp. 237–257.

14. See, e.g., Barry Sautman, "Anti-Black Racism in Post-Mao China," *The China Quarterly*, no. 138 (1994): 80–104. More recently, the journalist James Fallows informed Terry Gross, during his interview on the National Public Radio program *Fresh Air* (January 6, 2009), that the Chinese leadership were shocked that the United States citizens could elect Barack Obama, a black man, in its highest executive post. For them, it was placing the fate of the world in the hands of a racially inferior being. Consult: http://www.npr.org/templates/story/story .php?storyId=99039196.

15. See UNESCO report on school performance in predominantly black countries: *The EFA Global Monitoring Report*.

16. See Jonathan Kozol, *Shame of the Nation: The Restoration of Apartheid Schooling in America* (New York: Crown, 2005), pp. 28–29.

17. Simone Weil, "The Love of God and Affliction," in *The Simone Weil Reader*, ed. George A. Panichas (Kingston, RI: Moyer Bell, 1985), p. 443.

18. *Ibid*, pp. 440–441.

19. For discussion of some contemporary implications of this concept, see Lewis R. Gordon, "Can Men Worship?" sixth chapter of *Existentia Africana: Understanding Africana Existential Thought* (New York: Routledge, 2000), pp. 118–134.

20. Ellen K. Feder, "Lessons from Nietzsche: Reframing the Moral Questions in the Medical Management of Intersex," in *Heretical Nietzsche Studies*, a conference held at Temple University by the Philosophy Department and the Greater Philadelphia Symposium in Philosophy in April 2006.

21. Frantz Fanon, *Toward the African Revolution: Political Essays*, trans. Haakon Chevalier (New York: Grove, 1967), p. 8. This quotation is from the first chapter, "The 'North African Syndrome.'"

22. *Ibid.*

23. Sara Ahmed, *The Cultural Politics of Emotion* (New York: Routledge, 2004), p. 103.

24. *Ibid*, p. 106.

25. Frantz Fanon, *Black Skin, White Masks*, p. 11. These arguments against blaming the victims are familiar in the debate over the social welfare state. They are brought to the present in the rhetoric that followed Hurricane Katrina. See Giroux's *Stormy Weather* for an outline of them.

26. See Hannah Arendt, *Responsibility and Judgment*, ed. Jerome Kohn (New York: Schocken Books, 2005).

27. José Ortega y Gasset, *The Revolt of the Masses* (New York: W.W. Norton, 1932), pp. 71–74.

28. *Ibid*, p. 76.

29. *Ibid*.

30. See Carl Schmitt, *The Concept of the Political*, trans. with an introduction by George Schwab, with a foreword by Tracy B. Strong (Chicago: University of Chicago Press, 1996).

31. Carl Schmitt, *Political Theology: Four Chapters on the Concept of Sovereignty*, trans. George Schwab, foreword by Tracy B. Strong (Chicago: University of Chicago Press, 1985).

32. For a critique of the rejection of social welfare programs from a legal studies point of view, see the work of Joel Handler, *The Poverty of Welfare Reform* (New Haven, CT: Yale University Press, 1995) and *Social Citizenship and Workfare in the United States and Western Europe: The Paradox of Inclusion* (Cambridge, UK: Cambridge University Press, 2004).

33. Naomi Klein, "The Rise of Disaster Capitalism," *The Nation* (May 2005), p. 49. See also Klein, *The Shock Doctrine: The Rise of Disaster Capitalism* (New York: Metropolitan Books, 2007).

34. *Ibid*, p. 50.

35. *Ibid*, p. 51.

36. *Ibid*, p. 57.

37. *Ibid*, p. 58.

38. Kenneth Saltman, *Capitalizing on Disaster: Taking and Breaking Public Schools* (Boulder, CO: Paradigm Publishers, 2007).

39. Jean Comaroff and John Comaroff, "Law and Disorder in the Postcolony: An Introduction," in *Law and Disorder in the Postcolony*, ed. Jean Comaroff and John Comaroff (Chicago: University of Chicago Press, 2006), p. 41.

40. See, e.g., Thomas K. Gilhool, "The Right to an Effective Education: From *Brown* to PL 94-142 and Beyond," in *Beyond Separate Education: Quality Education for All*, ed. Dorothy Kerzner Lipsky and Alan Gartner (Baltimore, MD: Paul H. Brookes Publishing, 1989), pp. 243–253. See also Gary Orfield and Susan E. Eaton, *Dismantling Desegregation: The Quiet Reversal of "Brown v. Board of Education"* (New York: New Press, 1997), Gary Orfield and Carole Ashkinaze, *The Closing Door: Conservative Policy and Black Opportunity* (Chicago: University of Chicago Press, 1993), and Steven G. Brint, *Schools and Societies*, 2nd ed. (Palo Alto, CA: Stanford University Press, 2006), chapter 6.

41. Fanon, *Black Skin, White Masks*, p. 114.

42. This essay is included in Jean-Paul Sartre's *"What Is Literature?" and Other Essays*, ed. Peter Ungar (Cambridge, MA: Harvard University Press, 1988).

43. Fanon, *op. cit.*, p. 140.

44. These themes can be found in many works. See, e.g., Giroux, *Stormy Weather*; Kevin Bales, *Disposable People: New Slavery in Global*

Economy (Berkeley: University of California Press, 2000); Zygmunt Bauman, *Globalization: The Human Consequences* (New York: Columbia University Press, 1993) and *Wasted Lives: Modernity and Its Outcasts* (Cambridge, UK: Polity, 2004), and Comaroff and Comaroff, eds., *Law and Disorder*. See also, for discussion of the distinction between neoliberalism and neoconservatism, Wendy Brown, "American Nightmare: Neoliberalism, Neoconservatism, and De-democratization," *Political Theory* 34, no. 6 (2006): 690–714. Cf. also Lewis R. Gordon, *Disciplinary Decadence: Living Thought in Trying Times* (Boulder, CO: Paradigm Publishers, 2006).

45. We are referring to W.E.B. Du Bois's reflections in *The Souls of Black Folk: Essays and Sketches* (Chicago: A. C. McClurg, 1903). Discussions of his theoretical work abound. For one interpretation, see Lewis R. Gordon, "What Does It Mean to Be a Problem?" the fourth chapter of *Existentia Africana*. See also Reiland Rabaka, *W.E.B. Du Bois and the Problem of the Twentieth-First Century: An Essay on Africana Critical Theory* (Lanham, MD: Lexington Books, 2007) and Jane Anna Gordon's "Challenges Posed to Social Scientific Method by the Study of Race" in *A Companion to African-American Studies* (Malden, MA: Blackwell, 2006), pp. 279–304.

46. Elias Canetti, *Crowds and Power*, trans. Carol Stewart (New York: Farrar, Straus, and Giroux, 1984), pp. 242–246. Cf. also Marilyn Nissim-Sabat, *Neither Victim nor Survivor: Thinking Toward a New Humanity* (Lanham, MD: Lexington Books, 2009).

Notes for Chapter 2

1. For the existentialists, see Søren Kierkegaard, *The Concept of Anxiety*, trans. Reidar Thomte (Princeton, NJ: Princeton University Press, 1981) and Jean-Paul Sartre, *Being and Nothingness: A Phenomenological Essay on Ontology*, trans. Hazel Barnes (New York: Washington Square Press, 1956). For a similar discussion of the etymology of "monster," see Richard Kearney, *Strangers, Gods and Monsters: Interpreting Otherness* (New York: Routledge, 2002), p. 34.

2. See Aristotle's discussion of *eudaimonia* (blessedness) in his *Nicomachean Ethics* and cf. his discussion of the Unmoved Mover in his *Metaphysics*.

3. Richard Cavendish, *A History of Magic* (London: Arkana, 1987), p. 62. Cf. Kearney, *Strangers, Gods and Monsters*, p. 30. For a detailed study of monsters in religious contexts, see Timothy K. Beal, *Religion and Its Monsters* (New York: Routledge, 2002).

4. These were the Muslim Moors. The term, generically referring to many North African groups from late antiquity through the Medieval period, preceded the emergence of Islam in the seventh century. See, e.g., *The Golden Age of the Moors*, ed. Ivan Van Sertima (New Brunswick, NJ: Transaction Publishers, 1991).

5. Sebastian de Covarrubias Orozsco, *Tesoro de la lengua* (1611), quoted in and trans. David Nirenberg, "Race and the Middle Ages: The Case of Spain and Its Jews," in *Rereading the Black Legend: The Discourses of Religious and Racial Difference in the Renaissance Empires*, eds. Margaret R. Greer, Walter D. Mignolo, and Maureen Quilligan (Chicago: University Of Chicago Press, 2007), p. 79.

6. François Bernier, "A New Division of the Earth," from *Journal des sçavans* (April 24, 1684), trans. T. Bendyphe in *Memoirs Read Before the Anthropological Society of London*, Vol. 1, *1863–1864* (London: Trübner and Co, 1865), pp 360–64.

7. For more discussion, see, e.g., Benjamin Farrington, *What Darwin Really Said* (New York: Schocken, 1996).

8. For more discussion, see John Hick, *Evil and the God of Love*, rev. ed. (San Francisco: Harper SanFrancisco, 1978). The problem arises in other religions with a supreme deity as well; see Kwame Gyekye, *An Essay on African Philosophical Thought: The Akan Conceptual Scheme*, rev. ed. (Philadelphia: Temple University Press, 1995) and Beal, *Religion and Its Monsters*.

9. Simone Weil, "The God of Love and Affliction," in *The Simone Weil Reader*, ed. by George A. Panichas (Kingston, RI: Moyer Bell, 1985), pp. 438–468. The theme of externality, which we are here identifying as theodicean, is explored by other theorists of monstrosity as well. Cf. Beal, *Religion and Its Monsters*, pp. 39–40, as well as Richard Kearney, *Strangers, Gods and Monsters*, p. 31.

10. Weil, *ibid*, p. 468.

11. See Ernst Cassirer, *The Philosophy of Symbolic Forms: Volume 2: Mythical Thought*, trans. Ralph Manheim (New Haven, CT: Yale University Press, 1965), p. 29. For a critical exegesis of Cassirer's philosophy of mythic symbolic form, see chapter 4, "Myth as the Other of Logos or the Texture of the Real: The Presence of Meaning as the Meaning of Presence," in S. G. Lofts, *Ernst Cassirer: A "Repetition" of Modernity*, foreword by John Michael Krois (Albany: State University of New York Press, 2000), pp. 85–124.

12. Ernst Cassirer, *An Essay on Man* (New Haven, CT: Yale University Press, 1944), pp. 31–32.

13. Claude Lévi-Strauss, *Structural Anthropology*, trans. Claire Jacobson and Brooke Grundfest Schoepf (New York: Basic Books, 1963), p. 203.

14. *Ibid*, pp. 167–185. Cf. also Cavendish, *A History of Myth*, p. 2.

15. Lévi-Strauss, "The Structural Study of Myth," in *Structural Anthropology*, p. 230.

16. Cavendish, *A History of Magic*, p. 42. The authors are aware of this observation with the Jewish injunctions behind our use of the term G-d.

17. *Ibid*, p. 55.

18. *Ibid*, p. 1.

19. Peter Caws, *Structuralism* (Atlantic Highlands, NJ: Humanities Press, 1988), p. 25.

20. Many have argued such, and they are not all from the structuralist approach. See, e.g., Karl Jaspers, *Philosophy of Existence*, trans. R. F. Grabau (Philadelphia: University of Pennsylvania Press, 1971), and Leszek Kołakowski, *The Presence of Myth*, trans. A. Czerniawski, New Ed., (Chicago: University of Chicago Press, Chicago, 2001), and for a more succinct formulation of this argument by Claude Lévi-Strauss, see his *Myth and Meaning: Cracking the Code of Culture*, with a new foreword by Wendy Doniger (New York: Schocken, 1995). Cf. also, of course, Roland Barthes, *Mythologies*, trans. Annette Leavers (New York: Hill and Wang, 1972).

21. Peter Caws, "Sartrean Structuralism?," in *The Cambridge Companion to Sartre*, ed. Christina Howells (Cambridge, UK: Cambridge University Press, 1992), p. 305.

22. This richness and fluidity is evident in the many excellent recent studies of monsters, such as Beal's, Kearney's, and many more, such as the authors gathered for the anthology, *Monster Theory: Reading Culture*, ed. Jeffery Jerome Cohen (Minneapolis: University of Minnesota Press, 1996). There is much affinity between our discussions and theirs, but we diverge on the status of the Other. Many of these authors work within the framework of the monster as negative projection through acts of self-purification. Our contention is that this is sometimes so, but there are those for whom the structure is neither of self nor Other. This distinction will be evident in our succeeding chapters, but in general, we do meet with these authors in agreement that in many cases, there is the projected negative self, a self that is, as Beal argued, in a struggle with chaos and order.

23. For a discussion of the archaeology and study of these myths, see C. Finch, III, *Echoes of the Old Darkland: Themes from the African Eden* (Decatur, GA: Khenti, 1991).

24. Our readers are perhaps more familiar with the West Asian and East African myths mentioned here, more of which are discussed in Beal, *Religion and Its Monsters*. For the Australian ones, see, e.g., Charles E. Hully, *The Rainbow Serpent* (London, UK: New Holland Publishers, Ltd., 2000).

25. For a genealogy of the scapegoat, see Kearney, *Strangers, Gods and Monsters*, pp. 26–33. We will return and expand on this theme in chapter 4, below.

26. Although we focus on ocular metaphors in this chapter, concealment should not be read as exclusively so. In our fourth chapter, we turn to acts of silence and muting.

27. For more on Mami Wata, see Alex van Stipriaan, "Watramama/ Mami Wata: Three Centuries of Creolization of a Water Spirit in West Africa, Suriname and Europe," *Matatu: Journal for African Culture and Society*, nos. 27–28 (2005): 323–337 and *Sacred Waters: The Many Faces of Mami Wata*

and other Water Spirits in Africa, ed. Henry John Drewal (Bloomington, IN: Indiana University Press, forthcoming). Mami Wata is also echoed in contemporary brand culture, as the Starbucks logo reveals. The skeptical are encouraged to compare the images of Mami Wata and the Starbucks logo on Google Images: http://images.google.com/images?hl=en&client=firefox-a&channel=s&rls=org.mozilla:en-US:official&hs=ioU&q=Mami%20Wata&um=1&ie=UTF-8&sa=N&tab=wi and http://images.google.com/images?hl=en&client=firefox-a&channel=s&rls=org.mozilla:en-US:official&hs=EWp&q=Starbucks&um=1&ie=UTF-8&sa=N&tab=wi.

28. On the variety of meanings and various cultural interpretations of witches, see Elias K. Bongmba, *African Witchcraft and Otherness: A Philosophical and Theological Critique of Intersubjective Relations* (Albany: State University of New York Press, 2001). See also *Witchcraft and Magic in Europe*, eds. Bengt Ankarloo and Stuart Clark (Philadelphia: University of Pennsylvania Press, 2002) and Cavendish, *A History of Magic*.

29. See, e.g., Kwame Gyekye, *An Essay on African Philosophical Thought*. Cf. also Benjamin C. Ray, *African Religions: Symbol, Ritual, and Community*, 2nd. Ed. (Upper Saddle River, NJ: Prentice Hall, 2000).

30. R. Marie Griffith, *Born Again Bodies: Flesh and Spirit in American Christianity* (Berkeley, CA: University of California Press, 2004), p. 1.

31. The Public Broadcasting Station documentary is entitled *Capturing the Killer Croc* (2004), directed by Jean Michel Corillion and Vincent Munié. The title is a misnomer since Gustave was not caught. See also Michael McRae, "Gustave, the Killer Croc," *National Geographic Adventure* (March 2005): http://adventure.nationalgeographic.com/2005/03/gustave-crocodile/michael-mcrae-text/3.

32. Vered Lev Kenaan, *Pandora's Senses: The Feminine Character of the Ancient Text* (Madison: University of Wisconsin Press, 2008), pp. 48–49.

33. Arthur Schopenhauer, *The World as Will and Representation*, Vol. 2, trans. E. F. J. Payne (New York: Dover Publications, 1958), pp. 467–468.

34. See, e.g., *Lilith's Cave: Jewish Tales of the Supernatural*, selected and retold by Howard Schwartz (New York: Oxford University Press, 1991) and Roberto Sicuteri, *Lilith La Luna Nera* (Rome, Italy: Casa Editrice Astrolabio, 1980).

35. We return to this theme in our discussion of ruin in our fifth chapter, below.

36. The literature on antiblack racism is too vast to cite here. Most recent studies of race will illustrate our point. Even those who claim to be working beyond binaries of black and white often assert that binary as a subtext of analysis. For discussion of race and its modern emergence, see, e.g., Paul C. Taylor, *Race: A Philosophical Introduction* (Cambridge, UK: Polity, 2004), and for a theoretical study of specifically antiblack racism, see Lewis R. Gordon, *Bad Faith and Antiblack Racism* (Atlantic Highlands, NJ: Humanities Press, 1995) and Abdul JanMohamed,

The Death-Bound-Subject: Richard Wright's Archaeology of Death (Durham, NC: Duke University Press, 2005).

37. See Euripides, *The Cyclops*, trans. William Arrowsmith, in *Euripides II: "The Cyclops"and "Heracles," "Iphigenia in Tauris," and "Helen,"* ed. David Grene and Richmond Lattimore (Chicago: University of Chicago Press, 1952), pp. 35–36 (in the Greek, 580–590).

38. For a comprehensive discussion of vampires in cinema up until the new millennium, see M. J. Erreguerena Albaitero, *El mito del vampire: especificidad, origen y evolución en el cine* (Mexico City, Mexico: Plaza y Valdés, 2002). A future edition of this text will no doubt reveal a significant expansion of its already vast list of vampire films dating back to 1897.

39. Skeptical readers may wish to review the film, or simply consult this webite with a still from the motion picture: http://www.draculas .info/_img/gallery/bela_lugosi_as_dracula_75.jpg.

40. See Martin A. Monto, "Prostitution and Fellatio," *The Journal of Sex Research* (May 1, 2001): 140–145; and *Prostitution: On Whores, Hustlers, and Johns*, eds. James E. Elias, Vern L. Bullough, Veronica Elias, and Gwen Brewer (Amherst, NY: Prometheus Books, 1998). Oral sex is prominent as well in *Lost Souls* (New York: Dell, 1992), Poppy Z. Brite's brilliant, racialized, and queer portrait of "pure" and "mixed" vampires. We concede that racialization and queerness are redundant or at least doubly asserted in this context.

41. See Kant's *Critique of Judgment*, trans. W. Pluhar (Indianapolis, IN: Hackett, 1987), p. 174; or section 46, *Akademie* edition, p. 307.

42. *Ibid*, pp. 186–187; or section 49, *Akademie* edition, pp. 318–319.

43. *Ibid*, p. 177; or section 47, *Akademie* edition, p. 309.

44. For details of Kant's life, see Manfred Kuehn, *Kant: A Biography* (Cambridge, UK: Cambridge University Press, 2001).

45. Michael A. J. Howe, *Genius Explained* (Cambridge, UK: Cambridge University Press, 1999).

46. Oliver Sacks, *An Anthropologist on Mars: Seven Paradoxical Tales* (New York: Vintage Books, 1995), p. 225. Sacks explores the world of prodigies and geniuses, autistic and otherwise, through his relationship with Stephen Wiltshire, an autistic child who is also one of England's greatest recent prodigies; see pp. 188–243.

47. Roland Barthes, *Mythologies*, pp. 68, 70. For images of Einstein, we encourage readers to search his name in Google Images, which will take them to: http://images.google.com/images?hl=en&client=firefox-a&rls=org .mozilla:en-US:official&hs=iQ&q=Albert%20Einstein& um=1&ie=UTF-8&sa=N&tab=wi, and then type "young Albert Einstein," which will link the reader to: http://images.google.com/images?um=1&hl=en&client=firefox-a&rls=org.mozilla%3Aen-US% 3Aofficial&q=Young+Albert+Einstein& btnG=Search+Images. What is crucial is that it is the first set that appears with his name without the adjective "young."

48. See, e.g., Ira Katznelson, *When Affirmative Action Was White: An Untold History of Racial Inequality in Twentieth-Century America* (New York: W.W. Norton, 2006).

49. See Jean Comaroff and John Comaroff, "Alien-Nation: Zombies, Immigrants, and Millennial Capitalism," *The South Atlantic Quarterly* 101, no. 4 (Fall 2002): 779–805.

50. See, e.g., George Yancy's detailed, phenomenological description of a black male standing in an elevator with a white woman in his first chapter of *Black Bodies, White Gazes: The Continuing Significance of Race* (Lanham, MD: Rowman & Littlefield, 2008), "The Elevator Effect: Black Bodies/White Bodies," pp. 1–32. This phenomenon of negrophobic projection is also discussed in the sixth chapter of Frantz Fanon's *Black Skin, White Masks*, trans. Charles Lam Markman (New York: Grove Press, 1967), as a strange mixture of fear and desire. It is brought to the screen in a brilliant way, we contend, in the 1992 horror film *Candyman*, which brings these themes of fear of black talent, desire, and projection together in a story that culminates in the feared black as the white female protagonist's alter ego. She becomes, that is, what she has always been.

51. Friedrich Nietzsche, *The Will to Power*, trans. W. Kaufmann and ed. R. J. Hollingdale, with commentary by W. Kaufmann (New York: Vintage, 1967).

52. Weil, *op. cit.*, p. 445, is able to read similar phenomena without being nihilistic because of the gravitas of G-d: "Only blind necessity can throw men to the extreme point of distance, close to the Cross. Human crime, which is the cause of most affliction, is part of blind necessity, because criminals do not know what they are doing." A danger of Weil's view, however, is the eradication of responsibility through an over-expanded conception of ultimate innocence through an appeal to ignorance by way of the age-old problem of *akrasia*, of whether one ever knowingly commits evil. For a provocative recent discussion of *akrasia* and discourses of necessity, see Marilyn Nissim-Sabat, *Neither Victim nor Survivor: Thinking Toward a New Humanity* (Lanham, MD: Lexington, 2009), chapter 4.

53. *The Epic of Gilgamesh*, trans. Maureen G. Kovac (Palo Alto, CA: Stanford University Press, 1989).

54. See Arthur Schopenhauer, *The World as Will and Representation*.

55. See, e.g., Heidi Blake, "For the Dog That Has Everything: Botox and a Massage," *The Guardian* (15 July 2008): 3.

Notes for Chapter 3

1. See Frantz Fanon, *Black Skin, White Masks*, trans. Charles Lamm Markman (New York: Grove, 1967), chapter 5.

2. For a critical discussion of this prejudice in Jewish ethnography, see Walter Isaac, "Locating Afro-American Judaism: A Critique of White

Normativity," in *A Companion to African-American Studies*, eds. Lewis R. Gordon and Jane Anna Gordon (Malden, MA: Blackwell, 2006), pp. 512–542.

3. We would like to note our appreciation of an ongoing conversation with Lauren Bedell-Stiles on this point. Drawing on several recent horror films, he offered subtle observations about the ways in which these incite viewers to look with fresh eyes on what have otherwise become the mundane horrors of daily life. In more Gramscian language, postmodern creatures represent a significant break with earlier monsters in that they explore worlds that lack totalizing hegemonic values rather than ones characterized by battles over the normative substance that would organize these worlds.

4. Mary Shelley, *Frankenstein or the Modern Prometheus*, (New York: Dover Thrift, 1994), pp. 86 and 91. The reference to Fanon here is from the last chapter of *The Wretched of the Earth*, trans. Constance Farrington (New York: Grove, 1963).

5. Mary Shelley, *Frankenstein*, p. 22.

6. *Ibid*, p. 30.

7. *Ibid*, p. 32.

8. *Ibid*, p. 34.

9. *Ibid*, p. 35.

10. *Ibid*, p. 78.

11. *Ibid*, p. 79.

12. *Ibid*, p. 80.

13. *Ibid*, p. 81.

14. *Ibid*, p. 93.

15. *Ibid*, pp. 84–85.

16. *Ibid*, p. 85.

17. See *Narrative of the Life of Frederick Douglass, Written by Himself*, ed. with an introduction by Houston A. Baker, Jr. (New York: Penguin, 1986), p. 84. It is striking that when both Shelley's and Douglass's books were first published respectively in 1818 and 1845, that both contained prefatory remarks attesting to their authorship. In the former case, these were written by Percy Shelley, in the latter by William Lloyd Garrison and Wendell Phillips. In both instances, there were incredulous readers who would not accept that the texts, especially their horrific themes and exemplary style, had not instead been the ruminations of their endorsers.

18. Shelley, *Frankenstein*, p. 94.

19. *Ibid*.

20. *Ibid*, p. 99.

21. *Ibid*, p. 100.

22. *Ibid*.

23. *Ibid*, p. 102.

24. *Ibid*.

25. *Ibid*. When most critics of pedophilia imagine it, these are the kinds of images that come immediately to mind.

26. *Ibid.*

27. *Ibid*, p. 103.

28. *Ibid.*

29. *Ibid*, p. 111.

30. *Ibid*, pp. 120–121.

31. *Ibid*, p. 121.

32. *Ibid.*

33. *Ibid*, p. 122.

34. *Ibid*, p. 165.

35. Fanon, *The Wretched of the Earth*, p. 36.

36. Frantz Fanon, *A Dying Colonialism*, trans. Haakon Chevalier, with an introduction by Adolfo Gilly (New York: Grove, 1965), p. 47.

37. Frantz Fanon, *Black Skin, White Masks*, p. 17.

38. Shelley, *Frankenstein*, p.155.

39. Fanon, *Black Skin, White Masks*, p. 69.

40. *Ibid*, p. 112.

41. *Ibid*, p. 115.

42. See Jacques Lacan, "The Mirror Stage as Formative of the *I* Function as Revealed in Psychoanalytical Experience," in *Ecrits: The First Complete Edition in English*, trans. Bruce Fink (New York: W.W. Norton, 2007), pp. 75–81. For a more detailed discussion of its relevance and critique in Fanon's work, see Lewis R. Gordon, "Through the Zone of Nonbeing: A Reading of *Black Skin, White Masks* in Celebration of Fanon's Eightieth Birthday," *The C.L.R. James Journal* 11, no. 1 (Summer 2005): 1–43.

43. Jean-Paul Sartre, "Black Orpheus," trans. John MacCombie, in *"What Is Literature?" and Other Essays*, ed. Peter Ungar (Cambridge, MA: Harvard University Press, 1988), 291–330.

44. Fanon, *Black Skin, White Masks*, p. 134.

45. *Ibid.*

46. Paget Henry, "Africana Phenomenology: Its Philosophical Implications," *The C.L.R. James Journal* 11, no. 1 (Summer 2005): 86–89.

47. Fanon, *op. cit.*, p. 232.

48. Mary Wollstonecraft, *A Vindication of the Rights of Woman* (Mineola, NY: Dover Thrift), 1996.

49. See Mary Wollstonecraft and William Godwin, *A Short Residence in Sweden and Memoirs of the Author of 'The Rights of Woman'* (London: Penguin Classics, 1987).

50. Mary Wollstonecraft, *A Vindication of the Rights of Woman*, p. 37.

51. *Ibid*, p. 75.

52. These comments can be found in the *Simone Weil Reader*, ed. George A. Panichas (Kingston, RI: Moyer Bell, 1985), pp. 292–293.

53. For a discussion of this, see Sibylle Fischer, *Modernity Disavowed: Haiti and the Cultures of Slavery in the Age of Revolution* (Durham, NC: Duke University Press, 2004). This impulse was similarly at work

in the idea of "Black Consciousness" around which much anti-apartheid activism in South Africa was organized. One can find a consideration of the category of the normal inspired by a similar spirit in David Ross Fryer's, "On the Possibilities of Posthumanism, or How to Think Queerly in an Antiblack World," in *Not Only the Master's Tools*, eds. Lewis R. Gordon and Jane Anna Gordon (Boulder, CO: Paradigm Press, 2006).

54. Gloria Anzaldúa, *Borderlands/La Frontera: The New Mestiza,* 2nd ed. (San Francisco: Aunt Lute, 1999).

55. This is particularly evident in the attacks on Jean-Jacques Rousseau's idea of the general will, a concept describing a tension and expectation at the core of democratic thought and practice, that citizens combine popular with reasonable willing. The general will, though occupying a sturdy place in the history of ideas, is believed by most readers and writers to be unquestionably unfeasible. For discussion, see Jane Anna Gordon, *Creolizing Political Theory: Reading Rousseau Through Fanon* (New York: Fordham University Press, forthcoming, 2010).

56. Such monsters can easily be compared with the tyrant or despot at the end of Rousseau's *Second Discourse*. See Jean-Jacques Rousseau, *Discourse on the Origins of Inequality (Second Discourse), Polemics, and Political Economy*, The Collected Writings of Rousseau, Vol. 3, ed. Roger D. Masters and Christopher Kelly (Hanover, NH: University Press of New England, 1992).

Notes for Chapter 4

1. See Euripides, *The Cyclops,* trans. William Arrowsmith, in *Euripides II: "The Cyclops" and "Heralcles," "Iphigenia in Tauris," and "Helen,"* ed. David Grece and Richmond Lattimore (Chicago: University of Chicago Press, 1952), pp. 580–590, and our discussion in chapter 2, above.

2. Although colonization precedes the twentieth century, we have chosen to focus on cinema of that century because of its influence over the images and widespread iconography that gave popular justification to political decisions and norms that preceded them and that set the grammar for their ongoing consequences.

3. The reader might recall our earlier mention of Frankenstein's creature moaning at the sight of his own reflection. What was striking about this moment was that he, who was so articulate about so many other themes, could not find words to express his own feelings about his physical ugliness. In other words, his groan was the exception to a rule of embracing and working at what he considered to be the godly art of speech.

4. The connection here between vampires and immigrants echoes our earlier discussion of *Dracula* and raises interesting questions about the status of children of immigrants who, because of their uninflected speech, can frequently pass as locals.

5. Although we are here focusing on cultural perceptions and political practices that construct groups of people as monsters, our use of the term *subaltern* draws upon Gayatri Spivak's formulations in Leon de Kock's "Interview with Gayatri Chakravorty Spivak: New Nation Writers Conference in South Africa," *A Review of International English Literature* 23, no. 3 (1992): 29–47 and the poststructural problematic of muteness in her famous essay, "Can the Subaltern Speak?" in *Marxism and the Interpretation of Culture,* ed. Cary Nelson and Lawrence Grossberg (Urbana: University of Illinois Press, 1988), pp. 271–316. For a critical discussion of the latter essay, see Warren Montag, "Can the Subaltern Speak and Other Transcendental Questions," *Cultural Logic* 1, no. 2 (Spring 1998): http://eserver.org/clogic/1-2/montag.html. It is not our contention that all subalterns are monsters, but that, for many, their efforts to assert their humanity is responded to as monstrous.

6. The story of Prospero and Caliban in Shakespeare's play is subverted in Africana postcolonial literature, where Prospero is read as the colonizer of Caliban's island. See, e.g., Paget Henry's *Caliban's Reason: Introducing Afro-Caribbean Philosophy* (New York: Routledge, 2000). As well, the prescience of Mary Shelley's work, which we have characterized as proto-postcolonial, here emerges more fully. She anticipated what much political struggle has achieved more than a century later—a world in which "monsters" speak for themselves about the world that brought them into being.

7. See Paul Gilroy, *Postcolonial Melancholia* (New York: Columbia University Press, 2006).

8. Carol Pateman, "The Settler Contract," in Carol Pateman and Charles Mills, *Contract and Domination* (Cambridge, UK: Polity, 2007), chapter 2.

9. Examples of this first requirement can be found in John Locke's *Second Treatise of Government* (Indianapolis: Hackett, 1980). When explaining pre-contractual property, or periods when all the land was held in common and labor alone entitled one to it, Locke writes, "in the beginning, the whole world was America" (Chapter V, § 49). He goes on to explain that industry as evidenced by domesticated agricultural land was seemingly absent in what would become the American colonies. For more discussion of English conceptions of civilization as the cultivation of land, see Jill Lepore, *The Name of War: King Philip's War and the Origins of American Identity* (New York: Vintage Books, 1998), chapter 3.

10. For a more detailed discussion of *Worcester v. Georgia,* see Rogers M. Smith, *Civic Ideals: Conflicting Visions of Citizenship in U.S. History* (New Haven, CT: Yale University Press, 1999), pp. 238–239. He suggests that the decision depicted the tribes as examples of Emmerich de Vattel's "dependent 'tributary' or 'feudatory' states" that exchanged some of their sovereignty for the protection of a stronger state.

11. Soon after, in 1849, the main government office in charge of dealings with Native Americans, the Bureau of Indian Affairs, was moved

from the War Department into the new Interior Department, "indicating that the tribes now posed the challenge of development, not conquest." Rogers Smith, *Civic Ideals*, pp. 236–237.

12. Pateman, *op. cit.*, p. 78. This problem of those who either cannot or will not consent to what are framed as democratically conceived social contracts that pertain to them is a problem that runs throughout this tradition. Thomas Hobbes had easily dispensed with this objection when he argued that the consent of the vanquished—whose choice amounted to consenting to the terms of the new sovereign or death—could legitimately be presented as a choice. Locke's effort turned on combining the civilizational arguments to which we have already referred along with the distinction between full and express and tacit and partial members. Rousseau, who attempted most rigorously to honor a coherent view of consent, insisted that while opponents of an original contract did not violate it, that they could not be forced to be included in it. Their refusal would make them foreigners rather than citizens. Once the state was constituted, however, if a free state—one in which inhabitants were not kept by force—their residency implied consent. See *On the Social Contract*, p. 205.

13. What constitutes "civilized speech" has been contested since the sixteenth century. Consider, for example, Bartolomé de Las Casas's account of his refutation of the arguments of Juan Ginés de Sepúlveda concerning whether the Catholic Church could claim jurisdiction in the Spanish New World colonies over "the barbarians" who lived there. Las Casas considered each standing theological and colloquial definition of "the barbarian" in turn. The second of these included those "who do not have a written language that corresponds to the spoken one, as the Latin language does with ours, and therefore do not know how to express in it what they mean." Las Casas rejected this claim, pointing to the existence of precisely such a written language as well as countless other outward signs of civilization among Native Americans. He insisted that it was marauding Spanish conquistadores who had chosen to be Christians, and therefore taken on its commandments as their own, who were heretics and barbarous persons deserving of sanction and punishment by the Church. See Bartolomé de Las Casas, *In Defense of the Indians*, trans. Stafford Poole, C.M., foreword by Martin E. Marty (Dekalb: Northern Illinois University Press, 1992), p. 30.

14. Among the goals in Spivak's famous essay was a defense of Derridian deconstruction over Foucauldian and Deleuzian poststructuralism. She argues that "Derrida marks radical critique with the danger of appropriating the other by assimilation. He reads catachresis at the origin. He calls for a rewriting of the utopian structural impulse as 'rendering delirious that interior voice that is the voice of the other in us.' I must here acknowledge a long-term usefulness in Jacques Derrida, which I seem no longer to find in the authors of *The History of Sexuality* and *Mille Plateau*." Gayatri Chakravorty Spivak, "Can the Subaltern Speak?," in *Marxism and the Interpretation of Culture*, ed. Cary Nelson and

Lawrence Grossberg (Urbana: University of Illinois Press, 1988), p. 308. Our discussion of monstrosity addresses disgust, expulsion, rejections, and repulsion instead of assimilation, although some of the mechanisms of appropriation and assimilation emerge in ironic ways, as the reader will see in our discussions of exotic play and hybridity below.

15. See Jan Van Pieterse, *White on Black: Images of Africa and Blacks in Western Popular Culture* (New Haven, CT: Yale University Press, 1995), pp. 57–63.

16. Nelson Maldonado-Torres, *Against War: Views from the Underside of Modernity* (Durham, NC: Duke University Press, 2007), p. 239.

17. Rousseau, *On the Social Contract*, p. 146.

18. In other words, we here reject Carl von Clausewitz's claim that "War is nothing but a continuation of political intercourse with a mixture of other means ... [It is] a mere instrument of politics." See his *On War*, trans. Col. J.J. Graham. New and Revised edition with Introduction and Notes by Col. F.N. Maude, in Three Volumes (London: Kegan Paul, Trench, Trubner & C., 1918), Vol. 3, Chapter B, "War as an Instrument of Policy."

19. See Ortega y Gasset's *Revolt of the Masses*, p. 152.

20. Hannah Arendt, *The Human Condition* (Chicago: University of Chicago Press, 1958), pp. 7 and 175–176.

21. Agamben claims that the state of exception represented by the "sacred man" has increasingly become the rule in modern states that regularly suspend democratic rules of governance. Henry Giroux adds subtlety to this claim in his own exploration of Hurricane Katrina, when he insists that although states of emergency have increasingly become the norm of neoconservative politics, that not all lives are treated as equally disposable; those most readily allowed to suffer and die are those who are already marginalized by historic lines of race and class inequality. See Giorgio Agamben, *Homo Sacer: Sovereign Power and Bare Life*, trans. Daniel Heller-Roazen (Palo Alto: Stanford University Press, 1998), p. 8; and *State of Exception*, trans. Kevin Attell (Chicago: University of Chicago Press, 2005), chapter 6; and Henry A. Giroux's *Stormy Weather: Katrina and the Politics of Disposability* (Boulder, CO: Paradigm Publishers, 2006), in particular, p. 21.

22. Recall here our earlier discussion of Ellen Feder's exploration of the shame of many intersex patients in the face of the difficulty they cause their physicians and Fanon's analysis of the frustration occasioned by the North African Syndrome. The trouble there, too, was that their circumstance promised no easy resolution.

23. This passage is from "The Ethics of the Negro Question" in *The Voice of Anna Julia Cooper* (Lanham, MA: Rowman and Littlefield, 1998), pp. 206 and 209.

24. For an exploration of colonized people as the damned and the damned as a political category of equal significance to more familiar ones including the proletariat, the bourgeoisie, see Nelson Maldonado-Torres, *op. cit.*, especially pp. 151, 159, 218.

25. One is reminded of this phenomenon when one hears education researchers who reject assessments of U.S. education as in crisis. They point to the many products of public elementary and high schools who are in elected offices or teaching in universities and frame troubled, failing schools as the radical anomalies.

26. One can compare here the readiness to offer university courses, to purchase, read, and listen to the "experiences" of people from marginalized groups rather than to study the thought that emerges from them. For further discussion of this, see chapter 2 of Lewis Gordon's *Existentia Africana: Understanding Africana Existential Thought* (New York: Routledge, 2000).

27. W.E.B. Du Bois's reflections on the contribution of African slaves to U.S. cultural life come to mind. See, in particular, *The Souls of Black Folk: Essays and Sketches* (Chicago: A. C. McClurg, 1903) and also Amiri Baraka's *Blues People: Negro Music in White America* (New York: Harper Perennial, 1999); Anténor Firmin's *Equality of the Human Races*, trans. Asselin Charles and introduction by Carolyn Fluehr-Lobban (New York: Routledge, 2000); and Frantz Fanon, "Racism and Culture" in *Toward the African Revolution*, trans. Haakon M. Chevalier (New York: Grove, 1967), pp. 29–44.

28. Søren Kierkegaard, *Either/Or*, Vol. I, trans. David F. Swenson and Lillian Marvin Swenson, with revisions and a foreword by Howard A. Johnson (Princeton, NJ: Princeton University Press, 1959), p. 19.

29. Michael Alexander, *Jazz Age Jews* (Princeton, NJ: Princeton University Press, 2003).

30. *Ibid*, p. 149.

31. We place "white" in quotation marks and before "Jewish" to stress that not all Jews are white, and in some interpretations, *no* Hebrews or born Jews understood in their historical racial-ethnic history are white. Discussions in this regard are many, but see, e.g., Karen Brodkin, *How Jews Became White Folks and What That Says About Race in America* (New Brunswick, NJ: Rutgers University Press, 1999); Diane Tobin, Gary A. Tobin, and Scott Rubin, *In Every Tongue: The Racial & Ethnic Diversity of the Jewish People* (San Francisco: Institute for Jewish & Community Research, 2005); Walter Isaac, "Locating Afro-American Judaism: A Critique of White Normativity," in *A Companion to African-American Studies*, ed. Lewis R. Gordon and Jane Anna Gordon (Malden, MA: Blackwell, 2006), pp. 512–542; and Eric L. Goldstein, *The Price of Whiteness: Jews, Race, and American Identity* (Princeton, NJ: Princeton University Press, 2007).

32. Alexander, *Jazz Age Jews*, p. 171.

33. *Ibid*.

34. *Ibid*.

35. *Ibid*, p. 179.

36. For discussion of this conflict and the discourses governing it, see Jane Anna Gordon, *Why They Couldn't Wait: A Critique of the*

Black–Jewish Conflict over Community Control in Ocean Hill-Brownsville, 1967–1971 (New York: RoutledgeFalmer, 2001).

37. Recall our previous discussion of Carole Pateman. Efforts to coerce consent continue and change with shifting political circumstances, from an effort to make illegitimate foundations legitimate, to encouraging native and black participation in disavowing the failures to do so.

38. Consider here Steve Biko's defense of the need for black-run student anti-apartheid organizations and his criticisms of most white liberals. He suggested that white students who participated in student activism were able to have it both ways: simply by being born white in South Africa a substantially higher quality of life was available to them. Still, their participation in anti-apartheid organizations enabled them to feel that they were different from other, less critical whites and to move among them as if they were ethically and morally superior. See *I Write What I Like*, particularly "Black Souls in White Skins?"

39. See Irving Kristol's autobiography, *Neoconservatism: The Autobiography of an Idea* (New York: Free Press, 1995) and Houston Baker's critical discussion of it in Baker's *Betrayal: How Black Intellectuals Have Abandoned the Ideals of the Civil Rights Era* (New York: Columbia University Press, 2008), pp. 52–54, 60–61.

40. For a more developed discussion of this form of exoticism, see Lewis R. Gordon, *Bad Faith and Antiblack Racism* (Atlantic Highlands, NJ: Humanities Press, 1995), pp. 117–123.

41. Jean Comaroff and John Comaroff, "Law and Disorder in the Postcolony: An Introduction," in *Law and Disorder in the Postcolony*, ed. Jean Comaroff and John Comaroff (Chicago: University of Chicago Press, 2006), p. 31.

42. Peter Caws, "Sartrean Structuralism?" in *The Cambridge Companion to Sartre*, ed. Christina Howells (Cambridge, UK: Cambridge University Press, 1992), p. 296.

43. Elaine Scarry, *The Body in Pain: The Making and Unmaking of the World* (New York: Oxford University Press, 1987), p. 56.

44. *Ibid*, p. 35.

45. *Ibid*, p. 29.

46. *Ibid*, pp. 37–38.

47. Joshua Comaroff, "Terror and Territory: Guantánamo and the Space of Contradiction," *Public Culture* 19, no. 2 (2007): 383.

48. *Ibid*, pp. 384–385.

49. Aimé Césaire, *Discourse on Colonialism*, trans. Joan Pinkham, with an introduction by Robin D. G. Kelley (New York: Monthly Review Press, 2000), p. 41. See also Nelson Maldonado-Torres, *Against War*, chapter 1: "From Liberalism to Hitlerism: Tracing the Origins of Violence and War," pp. 23–51.

50. Saint Augustine made exactly this claim centuries ago when he insisted that all war, even evil war or war preempted by the iniquitous, was undertaken in the name of some peace; see Book XIX, Chapter 12

of *The City of God*, trans. Marcus Doas, with an introduction by Thomas Merton (New York: Modern Library, 1950).

51. Joshua Comaroff, "Terror and Territory," p. 402.

52. Booker Taliaferro Washington, "Atlanta Exposition Address, September 18, 1895," in *The Booker T. Washington Papers*, ed. Louis R. Harlan et al., vol. 3 (Urbana: University of Illinois Press, 1974), pp. 584–587.

53. There were a quarter of a million people at the event, and, adding television and radio coverage, documentaries, translations, and subsequent discussions worldwide, millions if not billions. For a history, see Juan Williams, *Eyes on the Prize: America's Civil Rights Years, 1954–1965* (New York: Viking, 1987).

54. Corey D. B. Walker, *A Noble Fight: African American Freemasonry and the Struggle for Democracy in America* (Urbana: University of Illinois Press, 2008), p. 24.

55. This move has required a radical act of forgetting depictions of King in his day as divisive and violent. Many advocates of the Black Power movement framed its militancy as a response to the failure to heed the divine warning of more integrationist approaches, ones that had framed racism in the U.S. as a tenacious anomaly that the best of American principles and politics contradicted.

56. For a recent history of Du Bois and Robeson and their relationship with each other, see Murali Balaji, *Professor and the Pupil: The Politics of W.E.B. Du Bois and Paul Robeson* (New York: National Books, 2007).

57. *The Autobiography of Malcolm X*, as told by Alex Haley (New York: Ballantine Books, 1964), p. 381.

58. For more discussion of King's influences, see Greg Moses, *Revolution of Conscience: Martin Luther King, Jr., and the Philosophy of Nonviolence*, foreword by Leonard Harris (New York: The Guilford Press, 1997). For an excellent recent discussion of Thurman's thought, see James Bryant and Paget Henry, "From the Pattern to Being: Howard Thurman and and Africana Phenomenology," *The C.L.R. James Journal* 12, no. 1 (Spring 2006): 61–84. The documentary history of white, especially mob violence on blacks, is widely available. See, e.g. *Witnessing Lynching: American Writers Respond*, ed. Anne P. Rice, foreword by Michele Wallace (New Brunswick, NJ: Rutgers University Press, 2003), especially, for additional references, the bibliography of documentary texts.

59. See the first chapter of Frantz Fanon, *Les Damnés de la terre*, préface de Jean-Paul Sartre (Paris: François Maspero éditeur S.A.R.L./ Paris: Éditions Gallimard, 1991; originally 1961). The debates on this chapter are many, including Hannah Arendt's famous polemic, *On Violence* (New York: Harvest Books, 1970).

60. Cf., e.g., William R. Jones, "Liberation Strategies in Black Theology: Mao, Martin, or Malcolm?," in *Philosophy Born of Struggle: Anthology of Afro-American Philosophy from 1917* (Dubuque, Iowa: Kendall/Hunt, 1983), pp. 229–241.

61. Obama's speech has been translated into many languages and is readily available worldwide, but see, e.g., "Obama Race Speech: Read the Full Text," *The Huffington Post* (March 18, 2008): http://www.huffingtonpost.com/2008/03/18/obama-race-speech-read-th_n_92077.html. We added "black" to refer to his father and "white" to refer to his mother since not all Kenyans are black and not all Irish are white, and there was a time in which no Irish were white.

62. King, similarly, had eventually distanced himself from Bayard Rustin, one of his mentors and organizers of the famous 1963 march on Washington. In addition to his remarkable civil rights work, which included the struggle for full employment, Rustin's background as a former member of the Communist Party USA, a socialist, and a homosexual became a liability to the version of King that was becoming more palatable to the American public. See, e.g., Larry Dane Brimmer, *We Are One: The Story of Bayard Rustin* (Honesdale, PA: Calkins Creek, 2007) and Mathew Forstater, "From Civil Rights to Economic Security: Bayard Rustin and the African American Struggle for Full Employment, 1945–1978," *International Journal of Political Economy* 36, no. 3 (Fall 2007): 63–74.

63. This challenge returns us again to our previous discussion of *Birth of a Nation*, a film that insisted that black political power could only be exercised as antiwhite revenge, that black people could not see and govern in pursuit of the common, American good.

64. See Søren Kierkegaard, *"Fear and Trembling"* and *"Repetition,"* ed. and trans. with introduction and notes by Howard V. Hong and Edna H. Hong (Princeton, New Jersey: Princeton University Press, 1983). For discussion, see *Kierkegaard in Post/Modernity*, edited by Martin Matuštík and Merold Westphal (Bloomington, IN: Indiana University Press, 1995) and Calvin O. Schrag, "Note on Kierkegaard's Teleological Suspension of the Ethical," in his *Collected Papers: Betwixt and Between*. (Albany, NY: State University of New York Press, 1994), pp. 27–32.

65. Henry Louis Gates Jr. and John Stauffer, "A Pragmatic Precedent," *The New York Times* (January 19, 2009): http://campaign.constantcontact.com/render?v=001Z53jn3_R531f7-Q_CjefgLMOWL7Rx H6gGKhe5jvtowGDWaEDksH9HEq2mLaorItVobQa2BVmhqEkT0PCO 8SisNSU81hT2fpTgx27knS3CcY%3D.

66. Richard Cavendish, *A History of Magic* (London: Arkana, 1990), p. 2. Cf., also, Max Weber's sociological considerations of this phenomenon in the charismatic politician: "Politics as a Vocation," in *From Max Weber: Essays in Sociology* (Oxford: Oxford University Press, 1946), pp. 77–128.

67. For Hannah Arendt on power, see her classic *The Human Condition*.

68. Sara Ahmed, *The Cultural Politics of Emotion* (New York: Routledge, 2004), p. 106; italics in the original.

69. *Ibid*, p. 108.

70. *Ibid*, p. 109, italics in original.

71. *Ibid*, p. 112, italics in original.

72. *Ibid*, p. 120.

73. For a rich discussion of the ways in which far-right American pro-business conservatives who initially supported the apartheid regime's resistance to liberal currents affecting their own country and the view that "communists are everywhere and liberals are their 'useful idiots'" made the transition to criticizing the same regime through the rearticulation of their original commitments, now as a libertarian attack on big government, see "From Paranoia to Privatopia by Way of Pretoria" in Thomas Frank's *The Wrecking Crew: How Conservatives Rule* (New York: Metropolitan Books, 2008).

74. See Lewis R. Gordon, "Phenomenology of Biko's Black Consciousness." In *Biko Lives!: Contestations and Conversations*, ed. Amanda Alexander, Nigel Gibson, and Andile Mngxitama (New York: Palgrave, 2008), pp. 83–93. See also Mabogo P. More, "Biko: Africana Existential Philosopher," same volume, pp. 45–68.

75. In "Biko Lives," Andile Mngxitama, Amanda Alexander, and Nigel C. Gibson describe contestations over Biko's memory in South Africa since 1994. The first, they argue, is expressed by members of the black business class who claim to be entitled to white wealth generated by colonialism and apartheid. The second, characteristic of political and bureaucratic classes, suggests that they have mobilized a version of Black Consciousness by privileging blackness in hiring selection so that job demographics better reflect those of the nation. It is in the third, in "everyday struggles of the black masses for dignity and freedom," they write, that the "living Biko finds expression," in *Biko Lives!*, edited by Alexander et al., p. 18.

76. As quoted in Hein Marais, *South Africa: Limits to Change, the Political Economy of Transition* (London: Zed Books, 1998), p. 146.

77. Thomas Frank, *The Wrecking Crew*, pp. 101 and 102.

78. *Ibid*, p. 121.

79. See, e.g., *Challenging Hegemony: Social Movements and the Quest for a New Humanism in Post-Apartheid South Africa*, ed. Nigel C. Gibson (Trenton, NJ: Africa World Press, 2006); and Ashwin Desai, *South Africa Still Revolting* (Johannesburg, SA: Impact Africa Publishing, 1999).

80. The frustrations of many blacks in the new South Africa expressed itself in xenophobic violence against black immigrants and visitors that compelled Nelson Mandela, while visiting England in celebration of his ninetieth birthday, to criticize their actions as an embarrassing moral failing. For work on how crime is read in the postcolonial societies of the new millennium, see *Law and Disorder in the Postcolony*, eds. Comaroff and Comaroff. For discussion of the shackdwellers' movement, see Nigel C. Gibson, "Introduction: A New Politics of the Poor Emerges from South Africa's Shantytowns," *Journal of Asian and African Studies* 43, no. 1 (February 2008): 5–18; Richard Pithouse, "A Politics of the Poor: Shack Dwellers' Struggles in Durban," *Journal of Asian and African*

Studies 43, no. 1 (February 2008): 63–94; Ashwin Desai, *The Poors of Chatsworth: Race, Class and Social Movements in Post-Apartheid South Africa* (Durban, SA: The Institute for Black Research/Madiba Publishers, 2000).

81. The shackdwellers' movement itself is highly articulate, full of very clear political proposals for what would enable the sign continuum of which they are apart to come to an end, as attested to in the following two published talks by one of its leaders, S'bu Zikode: "The Greatest Threat to Future Stability in Our Country Is the Greatest Strength of the *Abahlali baseMjondolo* Movement (SA) (Shackdwellers)," and "Sekwanele! Sekwanele! (Enough Is Enough!)," *Journal of Asian and African Studies* 43, no. 1 (February 2008): 113–125. Unlike the would-be vampires with whom we end this chapter, the shackdwellers want full citizenship and recognition as political agents, not monsters.

Notes for Chapter 5

1. Robert Ginsberg, *The Aesthetics of Ruins* (Amsterdam, The Netherlands: Rodopi, 2004), p. 387.

2. See Jean-Paul Sartre, *Being and Nothingness: A Phenomenological Essay on Ontology*, trans. Hazel V. Barnes (New York: Washington Square Press, 1956).

3. Ginsberg, *The Aesthetics of Ruins*, p. xvii.

4. *Ibid*, p. 7.

5. Arthur Schopenhauer, *The World as Will and Representation*, Vol. 2, trans. E. F. J. Payne (New York: Dover, 1958), pp. 634–635.

6. *Ibid*, p. 637.

7. Ginsberg, *The Aesthetics of Ruins*, p. 419.

8. *Ibid*, p. 439.

9. *Ibid*.

10. See Karl Jaspers, *Die Schuldfrage. Von der politischen Haftung Deutschlands* (Munich, Germany: Piper, 1965), available in English as *The Question of German Guilt*, with a new introduction by Joseph W. Koerski, S. J., trans. E. B. Ashton (New York: Fordham University Press, 2001).

11. Ginsberg, *op. cit.*, p. 439.

12. *Millennial Capitalism and the Culture of Neoliberalism*, eds. Jean Comaroff and John Comaroff (Durham, NC: Duke University Press, 2001).

13. See "Introduction," by Christopher Kelly, in *The Plan for Perpetual Peace, On the Government of Poland, and Other Writings on History and Politics, Collected Writings of Rousseau*, Vol. 2, trans, Christopher Kelly and Judith Bush, ed. Christopher Kelly (Hanover, NH: University Press of New England, 2005), p. xiv.

14. *Ibid*, p. 137.

15. *Ibid*, p. 125.

16. *Ibid*, p. 132.

17. Thomas Hobbes, *Leviathan*, Rev. Student Ed., ed. Richard Tuck (Cambridge, UK: Cambridge University Press, 1996).

18. Rousseau, *op. cit.*, p. 154.

19. Wandia Njoya, *In Search of El Dorado?: Immigration, French Ideals and the African Experience In Contemporary African Novels* (Saarbrücken, Germany: VDM Verlag Dr. Müller Aktiengesellschaft & Co. KG, 2008), p. 257.

20. See, e.g., Michael A. Fishbane, *Judaism* (San Francisco: HarperSanFrancisco, 1987); and Shaye J. D. Cohen, *The Beginnings of Jewishness: Boundaries, Varieties, Uncertainties* (Berkley: University of California Press, 1999).

21. For more discussion, see Marc Ellis, *Toward a Jewish Theology of Liberation: The Challenge of the 21st Century* (Waco, TX: Baylor University Press, 2004).

22. Richard Fenn, *The Secularization of Sin: An Investigation of the Daedalus Complex* (Louisville, KY: Westminster John Knox, 1991).

23. *Ibid*, p. 163.

24. For discussion, see Amanda Ruggeri, "$14 Billion Auto Bailout Bill Moves to Skeptical Senate After Passage in House," *U.S. News and World Report* (December 11, 2008): http://www.usnews.com/articles/news/national/2008/12/11/14-billion-auto-bailout-bill-moves-to-skeptical-senate-after-passage-in-house.html.

25. Fenn, *The Secularization of Sin*, p. 170.

26. *Ibid*, p. 178.

27. *Ibid*, p. 181.

Notes for Chapter 6

1. Dante Alighieri, *The Divine Comedy of Dante Alighieri*, vol. 1, *Inferno* (Toronto, Canada: Bantam, 1982), XXXIII, line 139.

2. Frantz Fanon, *Les Damnés de la terre*, préface de Jean-Paul Sartre (Paris: François Maspero éditeur S.A.R.L./Paris: Éditions Gallimard, 1961/1991), p. 376. Cf. *L'internationale*:

C'est la lutte finale / It's the final struggle.
Groupons-nous, et demain / Let us come together, and tomorrow
L'Internationale / the International
Sera le genre humain / will become the human race

3. Hannah Arendt, "Crisis in Education," in *Between Past and Future: Six Exercises in Political Thought* (New York: Penguin Classics, 1993), pp. 173–196.

◆

Bibliography

Agamben, Giorgio. 1998. *Homo Sacer: Sovereign Power and Bare Life*, trans. Daniel Heller-Roazen. Palo Alto, CA: Stanford University Press.
____. 2005. *State of Exception*, trans. Kevin Attell. Chicago: University of Chicago Press.
Ahmed, Sara. 2004. *The Cultural Politics of Emotion*. New York: Routledge.
Alexander, Michael. 2003. *Jazz Age Jews*. Princeton, NJ: Princeton University Press.
Alighieri, Dante. 1982. *The Divine Comedy of Dante Alighieri, vol. 1, Inferno*. Toronto, Canada: Bantam.
Ankarloo, Bengt, and Stuart Clark, eds. 2002. *Witchcraft and Magic in Europe*. Philadelphia: University of Pennsylvania Press.
Anzaldúa, Gloria. 1999. *Borderlands/La Frontera: The New Mestiza*. 2nd ed. San Francisco: Aunt Lute.
Arendt, Hannah. 1958. *The Human Condition*. Chicago: University of Chicago Press.
____. 1970. *On Violence*. New York: Harvest.
____. 1993. "Crisis in Education," in *Between Past and Future: Six Exercises in Political Thought*. New York: Penguin Classics, pp. 173–196.
____. 2005. *Responsibility and Judgment*, ed. Jerome Kohn. New York: Schocken.
Aristotle. 2001. *The Basic Works of Aristotle*, ed. Richard McKeon. New York: Modern Library.
Augustine, Saint. 1950. *The City of God*, trans. Marcus Doas, introduction by Thomas Merton. New York: Modern Library.
Baker, Houston. 2008. *Betrayal: How Black Intellectuals Have Abandoned the Ideals of the Civil Rights Era*. New York: Columbia University Press.
Balaji, Murali. 2007. *The Professor and the Pupil: The Politics of W.E.B. Du Bois and Paul Robeson*. New York: National Books.
Bales, Kevin. 2000. *Disposable People: New Slavery in the Global Economy*. Berkeley: University of California Press.
Baraka, Amiri. 1999. *Blues People: Negro Music in White America*. New York: Harper Perennial.

145

Barthes, Roland. 1972. *Mythologies*, trans. Annette Leavers. New York: Hill and Wang.

Bauman, Zygmunt. 1993. *Globalization: The Human Consequences*. New York: Columbia University Press.

_____. 2004. *Wasted Lives: Modernity and Its Outcasts*. Cambridge, UK: Polity.

BBC News. 2005. "At-A-Glance: Countries Hit," December 22: http://news.bbc.co.uk/2/hi/asia-pacific/4126019.stm.

Beal, Timothy K. 2002. *Religion and Its Monsters*. New York: Routledge.

Bernier, François. 1865. "A New Division of the Earth," from *Journal des sçavans* (April 24, 1684), trans. T. Bendyphe in *Memoirs Read Before the Anthropological Society of London*, vol. 1, *1863–1864*. London: Trübner and Co, pp. 360–64.

Biko, Steve Bantu. 2002. *I Write What I Like: Selected Writings*, ed. with a personal memoir by Aeired Stubbs, preface by Desmond Tutu, introduction by Malusi and Thoko Mpumlwana, new foreword by Lewis R. Gordon. Chicago: University of Chicago Press.

Blake, Heidi. 2008. "For the Dog That Has Everything: Botox and a Massage," *The Guardian* (15 July): 3.

Bongmba, Elias K. 2001. *African Witchcraft and Otherness: A Philosophical and Theological Critique of Intersubjective Relations*. Albany: State University of New York Press.

_____. 2006. *Dialectics of Transformation in Africa*. New York: Palgrave.

Bourdieu, Pierre. 1980. *The Logic of Practice*, trans. Richard Nice. Stanford, CA: Stanford University Press.

_____. 1997. *Pascalian Meditations*, trans. Richard Nice. Stanford, CA: Stanford University Press.

Brimmer, Larry Dane. 2007. *We Are One: The Story of Bayard Rustin*. Honesdale, PA: Calkins Creek.

Brint, Steven G. 2006. *Schools and Societies*, 2nd ed. Palo Alto, CA: Stanford University Press.

Brite, Poppy Z. 1992. *Lost Souls*. New York: Dell.

Brodkin, Karen. 1999. *How Jews Became White Folks and What That Says About Race in America*. New Brunswick, NJ: Rutgers University Press.

Brown, Wendy. 2006. "American Nightmare: Neoliberalism, Neoconservatism, and De-democratization," *Political Theory* 34, no. 6: 690–714.

Bryant, James, and Paget Henry. 2006. "From the Pattern to Being: Howard Thurman and and Africana Phenomenology," *The C.L.R. James Journal* 12, no 1: 61–84.

Camara, Babacar. 2008. *Marxist Theory, Black/African Specificities, and Racism*. Lanham, MD: Lexington.

Camus, Albert, 1954. *The Stranger*, trans. Stuart Gilbert. New York: Vintage.

Canetti, Elias. 1984. *Crowds and Power*, trans. Carol Stewart. New York: Farrar, Straus, and Giroux.

Cassirer, Ernst. 1944. *An Essay on Man.* New Haven, CT: Yale University Press.

———. 1965. *The Philosophy of Symbolic Forms: Volume 2: Mythical Thought,* trans. Ralph Manheim. New Haven, CT: Yale University Press.

Cavendish, Richard. 1990. *A History of Magic.* London, England: Arkana.

Caws, Peter. 1988. *Structuralism.* Atlantic Highlands, NJ: Humanities Press.

———. 1992. "Sartrean Structuralism?" in *The Cambridge Companion to Sartre,* ed. Christina Howells. Cambridge, England: Cambridge University Press.

Césaire, Aimé. 2000. *Discourse on Colonialism,* trans. Joan Pinkham, introduction by Robin D. G. Kelley. New York: Monthly Review Press.

Chambers, Timothy. 2006. "'They're Finding Food, but We're Looting?': A Two-Ethics Model for Racist Double Standards," *APA Newsletter on Philosophy and the Black Experience* 6, no. 1 (Fall): 5–7.

Clausewitz, Carl von. 2008. *On War,* trans. Colonel J.J. Graham, introduction and notes by Colonel F. N. Maude. Radford, VA: Wilder Publications.

Cohen, Jeffrey Jerome, ed. 1996. *Monster Theory: Reading Culture.* Minneapolis: University of Minnesota Press.

Cohen, Shaye J. D. 1999. *The Beginnings of Jewishness: Boundaries, Varieties, Uncertainties.* Berkeley: University of California Press.

Comaroff, Jean and John. 2000. "Millennial Capitalism: First Thoughts on a Second Coming," *Public Culture* 12, no. 2: 291–343.

———, eds. 2001. *Millennial Capitalism and the Culture of Neoliberalism.* Durham, NC: Duke University Press.

———. 2002. "Alien-Nation: Zombies, Immigrants, and Millennial Capitalism," *The South Atlantic Quarterly* 101, no. 4 (Fall): 779–805.

———. 2006. "Law and Disorder in the Postcolony: An Introduction," in *Law and Disorder in the Postcolony,* eds. Jean Comaroff and John Comaroff. Chicago: University of Chicago Press.

Comaroff, Joshua. 2007. "Terror and Territory: Guantánamo and the Space of Contradiction," *Public Culture* 19, no. 2: 383.

Cooper, Anna Julia. 1998. *The Voice of Anna Julia Cooper.* Lanham, MA: Rowman and Littlefield.

Cornell, Drucilla. 2007. *Moral Images of Freedom: A Future for Critical Theory.* Lanham, MA: Rowman & Littlefield.

Covarrubias Orozsco, Sebastian de. 1611. *Tesoro de la lengua,* quoted on p. 79 and trans. by David Nirenberg, 2007, "Race and the Middle Ages: The Case of Spain and Its Jews," in *Rereading the Black Legend: The Discourses of Religious and Racial Difference in the Renaissance Empires,* eds. Margaret R. Greer, Walter D. Mignolo, and Maureen Quilligan. Chicago: University of Chicago Press, pp. 71–87.

De Oto, Alejandro J. 2003. *Política del sujeto poscolonial.* Mexico City, Mexico: El Centro de Estudios de Asia y Africa, El Colegio de México.

Desai, Ashwin. 1999. *South Africa Still Revolting.* Johannesburg, South Africa: Impact Africa Publishing.

_____. 2000. *The Poors of Chatsworth: Race, Class and Social Movements in Post-Apartheid South Africa.* Durban, South Africa: The Institute for Black Research/Madiba Publishers.

Douglass, Frederick. 1986. *Narrative of the Life of Frederick Douglass, Written by Himself,* ed. with introduction by Houston A. Baker, Jr. New York: Penguin.

Drewal, Henry John, ed. Forthcoming. *Sacred Waters: The Many Faces of Mami Wata and other Water Spirits in Africa.* Bloomington: Indiana University Press.

Du Bois, W.E.B. 1903. *The Souls of Black Folk: Essays and Sketches.* Chicago: A. C. McClurg.

_____. 1938. *Black Reconstruction in America, 1860–1880.* New York: Harcourt, Brace.

Dussel, Enrique. 1981. *A History of the Church in Latin America: Colonialism to Liberation (1492–1979).* Grand Rapids, MI: William B. Eerdmans.

Elias, James E., Vern L. Bullough, Veronica Elias, and Gwen Brewer, eds. 1998. *Prostitution: On Whores, Hustlers, and Johns.* Amherst, NY: Prometheus Books.

Ellis, Marc. 2004. *Toward a Jewish Theology of Liberation: The Challenge of the 21st Century.* Waco, TX: Baylor University Press.

Erreguerena Albaitero, M. J. 2002. *El mito del vampire: especificidad, origen y evolución en el cine.* Mexico City, Mexico: Plaza y Valdés.

Euripides. 1952. *The Cyclops,* trans. William Arrowsmith, in *Euripides II: "The Cyclops" and "Heracles," "Iphigenia in Tauris," and "Helen,"* ed. David Grece and Richmond Lattimore. Chicago: University of Chicago Press.

Fallows, James, and Terry Gross. 2009. *Fresh Air,* January 6: http://www.npr.org/templates/story/story.php?storyId=99039196.

Fanon, Frantz. 1963. *The Wretched of the Earth,* trans. Constance Farrington, introduction by Jean-Paul Sartre. New York: Grove.

_____. 1967a. *A Dying Colonialism,* trans. Haakon Chevalier, introduction by Adolfo Gilly. New York: Grove..

_____. 1967b. *Black Skin, White Masks,* trans. Charles Lamm Markman. New York: Grove.

_____. 1967c. *Toward the African Revolution,* trans. Haakon Chevalier. New York: Grove.

_____. 1991/1961. *Les Damnés de la terre,* préface de Jean-Paul Sartre. Paris: François Maspero éditeur S.A.R.L./Paris: Éditions Gallimard.

Farrington, Benjamin. 1996. *What Darwin Really Said.* New York: Schocken.

Feder, Ellen K. 2006. "Lessons from Nietzsche: Reframing the Moral Questions in the Medical Management of Intersex," in *Heretical Nietzsche Studies,* a conference held at Temple University by the

Philosophy Department and the Greater Philadelphia Symposium in Philosophy.

Fenn, Richard. 1991. *The Secularization of Sin: An Investigation of the Daedalus Complex.* Louisville, KY: Westminster John Knox.

Finch, C., III. 1991. *Echoes of the Old Darkland: Themes from the African Eden.* Decatur, GA: Khenti.

Firmin, Anténor. 2000. *Equality of the Human Races,* trans. Asselin Charles, introduction by Carolyn Fluehr-Lobban. New York: Routledge.

Fischer, Sibylle. 2004. *Modernity Disavowed: Haiti and the Cultures of Slavery in the Age of Revolution.* Durham, NC: Duke University Press.

Fishbane, Michael A. 1987. *Judaism.* San Francisco: HarperSanFrancisco.

Forstater, Mathew. 2007. "From Civil Rights to Economic Security: Bayard Rustin and the African American Struggle for Full Employment, 1945–1978," *International Journal of Political Economy* 36, no. 3 (Fall): 63–74.

Foucault, Michel. 1977. *Discipline and Punish: The Birth of the Prison,* trans. Alan Sheridan. New York: Vintage.

Frank, Thomas. 2008. *The Wrecking Crew: How Conservatives Rule.* New York: Metropolitan Books.

Fryer, David Ross. 2006. "On the Possibilities of Posthumanism, or How to Think Queerly in an Antiblack World," in *Not Only the Master's Tools,* ed. Lewis R. Gordon and Jane Anna Gordon. Boulder, CO: Paradigm Press, pp. 227–242.

Gasset, José Ortega y. 1932. *The Revolt of the Masses.* New York: W.W. Norton.

Gates, Henry Louis, Jr., and John Stauffer. 2009. "A Pragmatic Precedent," *New York Times* (January 19): http://campaign.constantcontact .com/render?v=001Z53jn3_R531f7-Q_CjefgLMOWL7RxH6gGKhe 5jvtowGDWaEDksH9HEq2mLaorItVobQa2BVmhqEkT0PCO8Sis NSU81hT2fpTgx27knS3CcY%3D.

Gibson, Nigel C, ed. 2006. *Challenging Hegemony: Social Movements and the Quest for a New Humanism in Post-Apatheid South Africa.* Trenton, NJ: Africa World Press.

_____. 2008. "Introduction: A New Politics of the Poor Emerges from South Africa's Shantytowns," *Journal of Asian and African Studies* 43, no. 1 (February): 5–18.

Gilhool, Thomas K. 1989. "The Right to an Effective Education: From *Brown* to PL 94–142 and Beyond," in *Beyond Separate Education: Quality Education for All,* eds. Dorothy Kerzner Lipsky and Alan Gartner. Baltimore, MD: Paul H. Brookes, pp. 243–253.

Gilroy, Paul. 2006. *Postcolonial Melancholia.* New York: Columbia University Press.

Ginsberg, Robert. 2004. *The Aesthetics of Ruins.* Amsterdam, The Netherlands: Rodopi.

Giroux, Henry. 2006. *Stormy Weather: Katrina and the Politics of Dispos-ability.* Boulder, CO: Paradigm Publishers.

Godwin, William. 1976. *Enquiry Concerning Political Justice and Its Influence on Modern Morals and Happiness.* London, England: Penguin.

Goldstein, Eric L. 2007. *The Price of Whiteness: Jews, Race, and American Identity.* Princeton, NJ: Princeton University Press.

Goodsell, Charles T. 1988, "The Architecture of Parliaments: Legislative Houses and Political Culture," *British Journal of Political Science* 18, no. 3 (July): 287–302.

Gordon, Jane Anna. 2001. *Why They Couldn't Wait: A Critique of the Black-Jewish Conflict over Community Control in Ocean Hill-Brownsville, 1967–1971.* New York: RoutledgeFalmer.

_____. 2006. "Challenges Posed to Social-Scientific Method by the Study of Race," in *A Companion to African-American Studies,* ed. with introduction by Lewis R. Gordon and Jane Anna Gordon. Malden, MA: Blackwell, pp. 279–304.

_____. Forthcoming 2010. *Creolizing Political Theory: Reading Rousseau through Fanon.* New York: Fordham University Press.

Gordon, Lewis. 1999/1995. *Bad Faith and Antiblack Racism.* Atlantic Highlands, NJ: Humanities Press.

_____. 2000. *Existentia Africana: Understanding Africana Existential Thought.* New York: Routledge.

_____. 2005. "Through the Zone of Nonbeing: A Reading of *Black Skin, White Masks* in Celebration of Fanon's Eightieth Birthday," *The C.L.R. James Journal* 11, no. 1 (Summer): 1–43.

_____. 2006a. "Is the Human a Teleological Suspension of Man?: A Phenomenological Exploration of Sylvia Wynter's Fanonian and Biodicean Reflections," in *After Man, Towards the Human: Critical Essays on the Thought of Sylvia Wynter,* ed. Anthony Bogues. Kingston, Jamaica: Ian Randle.

_____. 2006b. *Disciplinary Decadence: Living Thought in Trying Times.* Boulder, CO: Paradigm Publishers.

_____. 2008a. "Phenomenology of Biko's Black Consciousness," in *Biko Lives!: Contestations and Conversations,* eds. Amanda Alexander, Nigel Gibson, and Andile Mngxitama. New York: Palgrave, pp. 83–93.

_____. 2008b. *An Introduction to Africana Philosophy.* Cambridge, England: Cambridge University Press.

Greer, Margaret R., Maureen Quilligan, and Walter D. Mignolo, eds. 2008. *Rereading the Black Legend: The Discourses of Religious and Racial Difference in the Renaissance Empires.* Chicago: University of Chicago Press.

Griffith, R. Marie. 2004. *Born Again Bodies: Flesh and Spirit in American Christianity.* Berkeley: University of California Press.

Gyekye, Kwame. 1995. *An Essay on African Philosophical Thought: The Akan Conceptual Scheme.* rev. ed. Philadelphia: Temple University Press.

_____. 1997. *Tradition and Modernity, Philosophical Reflections on the African Experience.* New York and Oxford: Oxford University Press.

Handler, Joel. 1995. *The Poverty of Welfare Reform.* New Haven, CT: Yale University Press.

_____. 2004. *Social Citizenship and Workfare in the United States and Western Europe: The Paradox of Inclusion.* Cambridge, England: Cambridge University Press.

Harris, Charlaine. 2008. *Dead Until Dark.* New York: Ace.

Henry, Paget. 2000. *Caliban's Reason: Introducing Afro-Caribbean Philosophy.* New York: Routledge.

_____. 2005. "Africana Phenomenology: Its Philosophical Implications," *The C.L.R. James Journal* 11, no. 1 (Summer): 79–112.

Hick, John. 1978. *Evil and the God of Love,* rev. ed. San Francisco: HarperSanFrancisco.

Hobbes, Thomas. 1996. *Leviathan,* rev. student ed., ed. Richard Tuck. Cambridge, England: Cambridge University Press.

Howe, Michael A. J. 1999. *Genius Explained.* Cambridge, England: Cambridge University Press.

Hully, Charles E. 2000. *The Rainbow Serpent.* London, England: New Holland Publishers.

Isaac, Walter. 2006. "Locating Afro-American Judaism: A Critique of White Normativity," in *A Companion to African-American Studies,* ed. Lewis R. Gordon and Jane Anna Gordon. Malden, MA: Blackwell, pp. 512–542.

JanMohamed, Abdul. 2005. *The Death-Bound-Subject: Richard Wright's Archaeology of Death.* Durham, NC: Duke University Press.

Jaspers, Karl. 1965. *Die Schuldfrage. Von der politischen Haftung Deutschlands.* Munich, Germany: Piper, 1965, available in English as *The Question of German Guilt.* New York: Fordham University Press, 2001.

_____. 1971. *Philosophy of Existence,* trans. R. F. Grabau. Philadelphia: University of Pennsylvania Press.

Jones, William R. 1983. "Liberation Strategies in Black Theology: Mao, Martin, or Malcolm?" in *Philosophy Born of Struggle: Anthology of Afro-American Philosophy from 1917.* Dubuque, IA: Kendall/Hunt.

Kant, Immanuel. 1987. *Critique of Judgment,* trans. W. Pluhar. Indianapolis, IN: Hackett.

_____. 1908. *Akademie* edition: *Kants gesammelte Schriften.* Vol. 5, ed. Wilhelm Windelband. Königlich Preußische Akademie der Wissenschaften. Berlin: Walter de Gruyter.

Katznelson, Ira. 2006. *When Affirmative Action Was White: An Untold History of Racial Inequality in Twentieth-Century America.* New York: W. W. Norton.

Kearney, Richard, 2002. *Strangers, Gods and Monsters: Interpreting Otherness.* New York: Routledge.

Kelly, Christopher. 2005. "Introduction" in *The Plan for Perpetual Peace, On the Government of Poland, and Other Writings on History and Politics, The Collected Writings of Rousseau, Vol. 2*, trans. Christopher Kelly and Judith Bush, ed. Christopher Kelly. Hanover, NH: University Press of New England.

Kierkegaard, Søren. 1959. *Either/Or*, vol. I, trans. David F. Swenson and Lillian Marvin Swenson, revisions and foreword by Howard A. Johnson. Princeton, NJ: Princeton University Press.

_____. 1981. *The Concept of Anxiety*, trans. Reidar Thomte. Princeton, NJ: Princeton University Press.

_____. 1983. *Fear and Trembling* and *Repetition*, ed. and trans. with introduction and notes by Howard V. Hong and Edna H. Hong. Princeton, NJ: Princeton University Press.

Klein, Naomi. 2007. *The Shock Doctrine: The Rise of Disaster Capitalism.* New York: Metropolitan Books.

Kock, Leon de. 1992. "Interview with Gayatri Chakravorty Spivak: New Nation Writers Conference in South Africa," *A Review of International English Literature* 23, no. 3: 29–47.

Kołakowski, Leszek. 2001. *The Presence of Myth*, trans. A. Czerniawski, new ed. Chicago: University of Chicago Press.

Kovac, Maureen G., trans. 1989. *The Epic of Gilgamesh.* Palo Alto, CA: Stanford University Press.

Kozol, Jonathan. 2005. *Shame of the Nation: The Restoration of Apartheid Schooling in America.* New York: Crown.

Kristol, Irving. 1995. *Neoconservatism: The Autobiography of an Idea.* New York: Free Press.

Kuehn, Manfred. 2001. *Kant: A Biography.* Cambridge, England: Cambridge University Press.

Lacan, Jacques. 2007. *Ecrits: The First Complete Edition in English*, trans. Bruce Fink. New York: W. W. Norton.

Las Casas, Bartolomé de. 1992. *In Defense of the Indians*, trans. Stafford Poole, C.M., foreword by Martin E. Marty. Dekalb: Northern Illinois University Press.

Lepore, Jill. 1998. *The Name of War: King Philip's War and the Origins of American Identity.* New York: Vintage.

Lev Kenaan, Vered. 2008. *Pandora's Senses: The Feminine Character of the Ancient Text.* Madison, WI: University of Wisconsin Press.

Lévi-Strauss, Claude. 1963. *Structural Anthropology*, trans. Claire Jacobson and Brooke Grundfest Schoepf. New York: Basic Books.

_____. 1995. *Myth and Meaning: Cracking the Code of Culture*, with a new foreword by Wendy Doniger. New York: Schocken.

Locke, John. 1980. *Second Treatise of Government.* Indianapolis, IN: Hackett.

Lofts, S. G. 2000. *Ernst Cassirer: A "Repetition" of Modernity*, foreword by John Michael Krois. Albany: State University of New York Press.

Maldonado-Torres, Nelson. 2007. *Against War: Views from the Underside of Modernity.* Durham, NC: Duke University Press.

Marais, Hein. 1998. *South Africa: Limits to Change, the Political Economy of Transition*. London, England: Zed Books.

Matuštík, Martin, and Merold Westphal. 1995. *Kierkegaard in Post/Modernity*. Bloomington: Indiana University Press.

McRae, Michael. 2005. "Gustave, the Killer Croc," *National Geographic Adventure* (March): http://adventure.nationalgeographic.com/2005/03/gustave-crocodile/michael-mcrae-text/3.

Mignolo, Walter. 2006. *The Idea of Latin America*. Malden, MA: Blackwell.

Mngxitama, Andile, Amanda Alexander, and Nigel Gibson, eds. 2008. *Biko Lives!: Contesting the Legacies of Steve Biko*. New York: Palgrave Macmillan.

Montag, Warren. 1998. "Can the Subaltern Speak and Other Transcendental Questions," *Cultural Logic* 1, no. 2 (Spring): http://eserver.org/clogic/1–2/montag.html.

Monto, Martin A. 2001. "Prostitution and Fellatio," *The Journal of Sex Research* (May 1): 140–145.

More, Mabogo P. 2008. "Biko: Africana Existential Philosopher," in *Biko Lives!*, eds. Andile Mngxitama, Amanda Alexander, and Nigel C. Gibson. New York: Palgrave, pp. 45–68.

Moses, Greg. 1997. *Revolution of Conscience: Martin Luther King, Jr., and the Philosophy of Nonviolence*, foreword by Leonard Harris. New York: Guilford Press.

New Zealand Herald. 2007. "Indian Ocean countries mark 2004 tsunami," December 27: www.nzherald.co.nz/tsunami-in-asia/news/article.cfm?c_id=500851&objcctid=10484368.

Nietzsche, Friedrich. 1967. *The Will to Power*, trans. with commentary by W. Kaufmann, ed. R. J. Hollingdale. New York: Vintage.

Nissim-Sabat, Marilyn. 2010. *Neither Victim nor Survivor: Thinking Toward a New Humanity*. Lanham, MD: Lexington.

Njoya, Wandia. 2008. *In Search of El Dorado?: Immigration, French Ideals and the African Experience In Contemporary African Novels*. Saarbrücken, Germany: VDM Verlag Dr. Müller Aktiengesellschaft & Co. KG.

Obama, Barack. 2008. "A More Perfect Union." Obama Race Speech: Read the Full Text, *The Huffington Post* (March 18): http://www.huffingtonpost.com/2008/03/18/obama-race-speech-read-th_n_92077.html.

Orfield, Gary, and Carole Ashkinaze. 1993. *The Closing Door: Conservative Policy and Black Opportunity*. Chicago: University of Chicago Press.

Orfield, Gary, and Susan E. Eaton. 1997. *Dismantling Desegregation: The Quiet Reversal of Brown v. Board of Education*. New York: New Press.

Pateman, Carol, and Charles Mills. 2007. *Contract and Domination*. Cambridge, England: Polity.

Pieterse, Jan Van. 1995. *White on Black: Images of Africa and Blacks in Western Popular Culture*. New Haven, CT: Yale University Press.

Pithouse, Richard. 2008. "A Politics of the Poor: Shack Dwellers' Struggles in Durban," *Journal of Asian and African Studies* 43, no. 1 (February): 63–94.

Rabaka, Reiland. 2007. *W.E.B. Du Bois and the Problem of the Twentieth-First Century: An Essay on Africana Critical Theory.* Lanham, MD: Lexington Books.

Ray, Benjamin C. 2000. *African Religions: Symbol, Ritual, and Community,* Second Edition. Upper Saddle River, NJ: Prentice Hall.

Reindhardt, Catherine. 2006. *Claims to Memory: Beyond Slavery and Emancipation in the French Caribbean.* New York: Berghahn.

Rey, Terry. 2007. *Bourdieu on Religion: Imposing Faith and Legitimacy.* London, England: Equinox Publishing.

Rice, Anne P., ed. 2003. *Witnessing Lynching: American Writers Respond,* foreword by Michele Wallace. New Brunswick, NJ: Rutgers University Press.

Roedigue, Christine M. 2002. "Media Coverage of the Events of 9/11": http://www.csulb.edu/~rodrigue/bldr911.html.

Rousseau, Jean-Jacques. 1987. *Basic Political Writings,* trans. Donald A. Cress, introduction by Peter Gay. Indianapolis, IN: Hackett.

_____. 1992. *Discourse on the Origins of Inequality (Second Discourse), Polemics, and Political Economy, The Collected Writings of Rousseau,* Vol. 3, eds. Roger D. Masters and Christopher Kelly. Hanover, NH: University Press of New England.

_____. 2005. *The Plan for Perpetual Peace, On the Government of Poland, and Other Writings on History and Politics, The Collected Writings of Rousseau,* Vol. 2, trans. Christopher Kelly and Judith Bush, ed. Christopher Kelley. Hanover, NH: University Press of New England.

Ruggeri, Amanda. 2008. "$14 Billion Auto Bailout Bill Moves to Skeptical Senate After Passage in House," *U.S. News and World Report* (December 11): http://www.usnews.com/articles/news/national/2008/12/11/14-billion-auto-bailout-bill-moves-to-skeptical-senate-after-passage-in-house.html.

Sacks, Oliver. 1995. *An Anthropologist on Mars: Seven Paradoxical Tales.* New York: Vintage.

Sadowski, Dennis, 2008. "Meeting Pope at Ground Zero Brings Tears to Sept. 11 Survivor," *The Catholic News Service* (April 29): http://www.catholicnews.com/data/stories/cns/0802366.htm.

Saltman, Kenneth. 2007. *Capitalizing on Disaster: Taking and Breaking Public Schools.* Boulder, CO: Paradigm Publishers.

Sartre, Jean-Paul. 1956. *Being and Nothingness: A Phenomenological Essay on Ontology,* trans. Hazel Barnes. New York: Washington Square Press.

_____. 1988. *"What Is Literature?" and Other Essays,* ed. Peter Ungar. Cambridge, MA: Harvard University Press.

Sautman, Barry. 1994. "Anti-Black Racism in Post-Mao China," *The China Quarterly,* no. 138: 80–104.

Scarry, Elaine. 1987. *The Body in Pain: The Making and Unmaking of the World*. New York: Oxford University Press.

Schmitt, Carl. 1985. *Political Theology: Four Chapters on the Concept of Sovereignty*, trans. George Schwab with foreword by Tracy B. Strong. Chicago: University of Chicago Press.

_____. 1996. *The Concept of the Political*, trans. with introduction by George Schwab, foreword by Tracy B. Strong. Chicago: University of Chicago Press.

Schopenhauer, Arthur. 1958. *The World as Will and Representation*, trans. E. F. J. Payne. 2 vol. New York: Dover.

Schrag, Calvin O. 1994. "Note on Kierkegaard's Teleological Suspension of the Ethical," in his *Collected Papers: Betwixt and Between*. Albany: State University of New York Press, pp. 27–32.

Schwartz, Howard. 1991. *Lilith's Cave: Jewish Tales of the Supernatural*. New York: Oxford University Press.

Senghor, Leopold. 2000. "What is 'Negritude'?" in *The Idea of Race*, ed. with introductions by Robert Bernasconi and Tommy L. Lott. Indianapolis: Hackett.

Sertima, Ivan van, ed. 1991. *The Golden Age of the Moors*. New Brunswick, NJ: Transaction Publishers.

Shakespeare, William. 2008. *The Complete Works of Shakespeare*, 6th ed., ed. David Bevington. New York: Longman.

Shelley, Mary. 1994. *Frankenstein or the Modern Prometheus*. Mineola, NY: Dover Thrift Edition.

Sicuteri, Roberto. 1980. *Lilith La Luna Nera*. Rome, Italy: Casa Editrice Astrolabio.

Smith, Rogers M. 1999. *Civic Ideals: Conflicting Visions of Citizenship in U.S. History*. New Haven, CT: Yale University Press.

Spivak, Gayatri Chakravorty. 1988. "Can the Subaltern Speak?" in *Marxism and the Interpretation of Culture*, ed. Cary Nelson and Lawrence Grossberg. Urbana: University of Illinois Press, pp. 271–316.

Stephens, Henry Morse, ed. 1982. *The Principal Speeches of the Statesmen and Orators of the French Revolution,1789–1795*, vol. II. Oxford: Clarendon Press.

Stipriaan, Alex van. 2005. "Watramama/Mami Wata: Three Centuries of Creolization of a Water Spirit in West Africa, Suriname and Europe," *Matatu: Journal for African Culture and Society*, nos. 27–28: 323–337.

Taylor, Paul C. 2004. *Race: A Philosophical Introduction*. Cambridge, England: Polity.

Tobin, Diane, Gary A. Tobin, and Scott Rubin. 2005. *In Every Tongue: The Racial & Ethnic Diversity of the Jewish People*. San Francisco: Institute for Jewish & Community Research.

UNESCO report on school performance in predominantly black countries: *The EFA Global Monitoring Report*.

Vedantam, Shankar, 2007. "Along with Grief, 9/11 Survivors Find Resolve," *The Washington Post* (September 10).

Walker, Corey D. B. 2008. *A Noble Fight: African American Freemasonry and the Struggle for Democracy in America.* Urbana: University of Illinois Press.

Ward, David, 2006. "Survivors of Tsunami Castigate Foreign Office," *The Guardian,* November 30.

Washington, Booker Taliaferro. 1974. "Atlanta Exposition Address, September 18, 1895," in *The Booker T. Washington Papers,* eds. Louis R. Harlan et al., vol. 3. Urbana: University of Illinois Press, pp. 584–587.

Weber, Max. 1946. *From Max Weber: Essays in Sociology.* Oxford: Oxford University Press.

——. 2002. *The Protestant Work Ethic and the "Spirit" of Capitalism and Other Writings,* ed., trans., and introduced by Peter Baehr and Gordon C. Wells. New York: Penguin.

Weil, Simone. 1985. *The Simone Weil Reader,* ed. George A. Panichas. Kingston, RI: Moyer Bell.

Willard, Charity Cannon. 1984. *Christine de Pizan: Her Life and Works.* New York: Persea Books.

Williams, Juan. 1987. *Eyes on the Prize: America's Civil Rights Years, 1954–1965.* New York: Viking.

Wollstonecraft, Mary. 1996. *A Vindication of the Rights of Woman.* Mineola, NY: Dover Thrift Editions.

Wollstonecraft, Mary, and William Godwin. 1987. *A Short Residence in Sweden and Memoirs of the Author of 'The Rights of Woman.'* London, England: Penguin Classics.

X, Malcolm. 1964. *The Autobiography of Malcolm X,* as told by Alex Haley. New York: Ballantine.

Yancy, George. 2008. *Black Bodies, White Gazes: The Continuing Significance of Race.* Lanham, MD: Rowman & Littlefield.

Zikode, S'bu. 2008. "The Greatest Threat to Future Stability in Our Country Is the Greatest Strength of the *Abahlali baseMjondolo* Movement (SA) (Shackdwellers)," and "Sekwanel! Sekwanele! (Enough Is Enough!)," *Journal of Asian and African Studies* 43, no. 1 (February): 113–125.

◇

Index

◇

About the Authors

Jane Anna Gordon teaches in the Department of Political Science and the Program in Jewish Studies at Temple University, where she codirects the Institute for the Study of Race and Social Thought and the Center for Afro-Jewish Studies. She is the author of *Why They Couldn't Wait: A Critique of the Black-Jewish Conflict over Community Control in Ocean-Hill Brownsville, 1967–1971* (Routledge, 2001), which was listed by *The Gotham Gazette* as one of the four best books recently published on Civil Rights, and co-editor of *A Companion to African-American Studies* (Blackwell, 2006) and *Not Only the Master's Tools* (Paradigm Publishers, 2006). Her latest book, *Creolizing Political Theory: Reading Rousseau Through Fanon*, is forthcoming with Fordham University Press.

Lewis Ricardo Gordon is the Laura H. Carnell Professor of Philosophy, Religion, and Jewish Studies at Temple University where he also codirects the Institute for the Study of Race and Social Thought and the Center for Afro-Jewish Studies; he is also the Jay Newman Visiting Professor of Philosophy of Culture at Brooklyn College. He is the author of several influential and award-winning books, such as *Bad Faith and Antiblack Racism* (Humanities Press,1995); *Fanon and the Crisis of European Man* (Routledge, 1995); *Her Majesty's Other Children* (Rowman & Littlefield, 1997), which won the Gustavus Myer Award for Outstanding Work on Human Rights in North America; *Existentia Africana* (Routledge, 2000); *Disciplinary Decadence* (Paradigm Publishers, 2006); *An Introduction to Africana Philosophy* (Cambridge UP, 2008); and his co-edited *A Companion to African-American Studies* (Blackwell, 2006), which was chosen as the NetLibrary eBook of the Month for February 2007. His other anthologies and co-edited books include *Fanon: A Critical Reader* (Blackwell, 1996), *Existence in Black: An Anthology of Black Existential Philosophy* (Routledge 1997), and *Not Only the Master's Tools: African-American Studies in Theory and Practice* (Paradigm Publishers, 2006). His next book, *"No Longer Enslaved, Yet Not Quite Free": Essays on Freedom, Justice, and the Decolonization of Knowledge*, is forthcoming with Fordham University Press.

166